Reflections on
Chinese Management Styles
and Business Ethics

Reflections on Chinese Management Styles and Business Ethics

EDITORS

Jitendra K. Das
Mathew Joseph

FORE School of Management
New Delhi

BLOOMSBURY
NEW DELHI • LONDON • OXFORD • NEW YORK • SYDNEY

BLOOMSBURY and the Diana logo are trademarks of Bloomsbury Publishing Plc
ISBN 978 93 82563 63 1
1 2 3 4 5 6 7 8 9 10

Bloomsbury Publishing India Pvt. Ltd
DDA Complex, LSC Building No. 4
Second Floor, Pocket C – 6 & 7, Vasant Kunj
New Delhi 110070
www.bloomsbury.com

Printed and bound in India

To find out more about our authors and books visit www.bloomsbury.com. Here you will find extracts, author interviews, details of forthcoming events and the option to sign up for our newsletters.

Contents

Foreword

I congratulate the FORE School of Management, New Delhi for taking the initiative in seriously studying the contemporary state of Chinese economy from a multi-dimensional perspective. The essays deal with subjects ranging from changes in the traditional business culture and the experience with infrastructure building on a massive scale, to specific aspects of the economic development, such as the way the Chinese responded to the global economic crisis. Interesting articles on the status of women and the nature of higher education have important implications for India. Based on the visit of scholars to China in October–November 2011, the articles present useful insights.

There are two compulsions which policy makers in China have grappled with in the recent years. One was conspicuously thrown into the forefront in course of the global crisis that the export-led, investment-based strategy of the 1990s and 2000s which achieved high growth rates and made China the world's second largest economy, had to be reoriented. As the articles in this book point out, the Chinese leadership was clearly aiming to expand domestic demand on a large scale so that the vulnerability to fluctuations in the world economy would be under control. The other compulsion is indicated in some of the articles, including those on 'Hukou' system, higher education and gender which point out that social inequality, regional disparity and environmental problems were generated in the reform process, and represent another set of problems.

The past decade of the regime led by President Hu Jintao and Premier Wen Jiabao was known for addressing the second, or the social and environmental compulsions and the XI Five Year Plan had emphasised these goals. The XII Plan which began in 2011, addressed the first compulsion as well, by focusing on the need for "transforming the pattern of development". But as the articles in this book suggest, the challenges persist despite successes in many spheres.

The discussion on business culture in our times takes the European business culture as the reference point. So the "*guanxi*" system of informal solidarity in China or the "*Marwari*" business values in India look deviant to many. As is pointed out, global business culture is a dynamic process incorporating different strands. Sun Tzu's '*Art of War*' influencing all business deals is an interesting way to look at the subject.

That the number of Chinese women entrepreneurs have grown during the reform period is a fact. It is also true that the number of women cadres in the CPC and the officials in the government at various levels is fairly high. However, as the contributions in this book show the women's share in the higher levels of political leadership is minimal. Even more important to note is the fact that, in many branches of the economy, women have lost jobs in large numbers in recent years.

Urban-rural migration is a major problem of developing economies. China's '*hukou*' system has indeed been an unfair system for the rural population. As the articles in this book points out, it has denied many basic facilities to the rural migrants to the cities even though there has been relaxation on the migration of people from the countryside.

Emergence of China on world stage has many possibilities. Does China seriously wish to restructure the world's financial system by staking a claim for its currency *renminbi* to become a world currency? Is it helping the BRICS process to democratise the world political economy? Many articles in this books give a number of useful ideas on this subject.

India-China economic relations are growing at a fast pace and are set to achieve the US$ 100 billion mark in trade volume by 2015. But, Indian expertise about the Chinese economy is still meagre. This book is a very welcome contribution to the growth of Indian scholarly work on the Chinese economy. I hope the FORE School will take more initiatives of this kind, and create a momentum for creative Indian scholarship on China.

Manoranjan Mohanty
Chairperson
Institute of Chinese Studies
8/17 Sri Ram Road
New Delhi–110054
E-mail: mmohantydu@gmail.com

Introduction

Jitendra K. Das and Mathew Joseph

The extraordinary growth of the Chinese economy—at an average rate of about 10 percent per annum, in the past three decades has resulted in China becoming the second largest economy in the world in 2010, overtaking Japan. The Chinese economy is tipped to overtake the US as the world's biggest economy by 2027, according to the latest estimates by Goldman Sachs. However, China faces huge challenges as the country attempts to recast its development model from an export-oriented, investment-led model of the past to a more domestic-consumption-oriented one for the future. Global crisis brought out very clearly that China can no longer rely on its past growth strategy to sustain its high growth rate in the future.

As part of the faculty development programme at the FORE School of Management, the faculty visited China during October–November 2011. During the visit, the faculty had a number of interactive sessions with scholars from the University of International Business at Beijing on the economy, infrastructure, trade, business environment and business culture of China. The visit helped the faculty to gain rich first-hand knowledge about China. After the visit, the faculty wrote articles on various aspects of China, based on their earlier research and the new China experience. These articles are included in this book.

The book is organized into three broad areas: China's business culture, infrastructure and the economy.

China's Business Culture

"Guanxi" in Chinese literally means "get connected," and in China to do business one needs to build "relationships." Hitesh Arora's paper examines *guanxi* as an instrument to conduct business in China. This is unlike western countries, where strangers can suddenly begin talking business after they are introduced by a third person. *Guanxi* implies that there is a minimum threshold level, below which strangers remain as strangers, and relationships are not possible. The article also analyses the existing literature on the influence of *guanxi* on corporate governance behaviour and management trust. More importantly, it describes how, in the context of Michael Porter's value chain system, through a strong *guanxi* network, firms can enhance their competitive advantage over rivals.

It is known that culture influences management styles, which includes conflict handling and negotiating styles. But, culture is not immutable and is influenced by changes in the internal and external political, economic and social milieu. While Confucianism is the backbone of Chinese culture, changes in Chinese culture have occurred due to other ancient philosophies, such as Taoism, Buddhism and Legalism. The article by Prachi Bhatt highlights the forces impacting changes in a distinct Chinese culture, and urges the need for further studies to understand the influences governing contemporary management styles.

Ambrish Gupta critically examines the Chinese management style and business ethics, as revealed from the studies by Zhenzhong Ma. It also brings out some practical lessons for Indian businessmen who have to deal with their Chinese counterparts.

Modern Chinese management has deep cultural roots. The article by Neetu Jain examines the extent to which contemporary Chinese management is influenced by international best practices.

The article by Anita Tripathy Lal brings out the Chinese way of doing business, which is somewhat different from global business practices. The article further attempts to understand typical Chinese business styles from an analysis of Chinese communication style, workplace mannerisms and business negotiations.

China being a nation with perhaps the highest propensity to save, it would be interesting to know how the Chinese invest in various financial products. Drawing from behavioural finance to explain the choice of savings instruments by Chinese households, the article by Shalini Kalra Sahi highlights the importance of culture in determining purchase of different financial products by them.

"The Art of War" written by Sun Tzu, the Chinese philosopher, thinker and mentor almost 2500 years ago, is a military treatise, but has long been recognized as having implications for business strategy. The article by Mohita G. Sharma interestingly attempts to extract business operations acumen out of the various citations from Sun Tzu's *Art of War*.

The article by Sanghamitra Buddhapriya narrates the incredible progress made by Chinese women from being just appendages of men in the mid-twentieth century, to successful business leaders and entrepreneurs today. This transformation happened due to successive constitutional and legal changes made after the Communist revolution. However, women continue to be grossly unrepresented at the political arena in China. For further advancement of women in China, the state driven initiatives have to be complemented by efforts from civil societies.

China's Infrastructure

We have heard of the legendary infrastructure building that is going on in contemporary China. Visitors to China marvel at the speed and scale of infrastructural projects in the country. The article by Qazi Asif Zameer provides a review of infrastructural growth in China by marshalling both positive and negative facts, and concludes that "all is not well" in the dragon's land.

Anupam Narula reviews the progress of higher education in both China and India. Although considerable strides have been made by both countries in higher education, the article further brings out the need for reforms in improving the quality and access of post-secondary education both in China and India.

The banks in both China and India escaped unscathed the global financial crisis. The article by Vinay Dutta examines the performance of commercial banks in both China and India coming out of the global financial crisis. The article also describes the various challenges faced by the banks in the post-crisis period.

The Chinese Economy

The global financial crisis of 2008 hit almost all the countries in the world, and every government took measures to counter the impact of the crisis. The article by Mathew Joseph considers the contrasting policy responses between China and India. While the Indian government responded by boosting domestic consumption through direct government spending, the Chinese government responded with higher domestic investments through bank lending. The former resulted in a drop of the productive capacity of the economy, and an increase in the fiscal deficit. And the latter, while raising the productive capacity of the economy, led to a weakening of the banks by raising their non-performing assets.

Does the Chinese renminbi deserve the reserve-currency status? This is the question which is increasingly being asked in the context of the rapidly rising Chinese economy and trade. The article by Himanshu Joshi discusses the benefits and costs of the currency getting the reserve currency status, and examines the factors that will determine Chinese renminbi assuming that role in the future.

The "*hukou*" system in China is basically a system of registration of households, dividing the Chinese population into agriculturists and non-agriculturists. The article by Neeraj Kumar examines how a system aimed at "maintaining social order, protect citizens' rights and benefits" over the years, created a vast pool of cheap labour for the industrialization of China, on the one hand, and created inequalities in social and regional development, leading to social tensions, on the other.

The amazing growth story of China is based on government statistics. However, many independent observers have cast doubts on the veracity of the government data in China. Kanhaiya Singh brings together some of the very important findings about the truth of Chinese government statistics.

It is hoped that the articles in this book will provide interesting insights about the Chinese economy and business, and stimulate discussions about the role of China in the evolving international economic order.

A Competitive Advantage Strategy in China: *Guanxi*

Hitesh Arora

FORE School of Management, New Delhi
E-mail: hitesh@fsm.ac.in

ABSTRACT

If used strategically, Guanxi has the potential to transform products, processes, competition and business itself. It can lead to substantial and sustainable competitive advantages. The article develops an understanding of Guanxi in the realm of business. The aim of the article is to discuss Guanxi as a strategy for gaining competitive advantage in Chinese markets. The firms that appropriately apply this strategy can enhance their chances of success in China.

Keywords: Guanxi, Competitive Advantage, Chinese Management, Value Chain.

Introduction

Starting a new business in China (a planned economy) is not easy. Every firm (local, state-owned or foreign) operating in China, faces institutional barriers. A common way to help firms circumvent institutional barriers in China is the use of *Guanxi* (Gu *et al.*, 2008). *Guanxi* or developing close relationships is considered a prerequisite for overcoming various difficulties like accessing government controlled resources, information, credit etc. In fact, Chinese business behaviour has always revolved around *Guanxi* for many centuries (Wong *et al.*, 2010). *Guanxi*, identified as one of the major dynamics and requisite for survival in Chinese society, is different from Western relationships in terms of (i) legality, and (ii) management philosophy. Chinese relationships rely on morality and places emphasis on the 'heart' (Westerners place emphasis on the 'mind') (Wong *et al.*, 2007).

Though, the role of *Guanxi* is well recognized in Chinese business and academics, a few have attempted to investigate its managerial implications. This article looks at *guanxi* in the light of its managerial implications as a competitive advantage strategy. The purpose of the article is to emphasize that managers can obtain substantial and sustainable competitive advantages through *guanxi*. Firms using *guanxi* as a business strategy, would find themselves placed at a competitive advantage compared to those who do not.

The rest of the article is organized as follows. Section II examines the meaning, nature and dimensions of *guanxi*. Section III throws light on various managerial perspectives of *guanxi* in earlier studies. Section IV shows how managers can weigh their *guanxi* network to turn it to their advantage. Section V are the conclusions.

Guanxi: Meaning, Nature and Dimensions

Although, numerous authors have defined *'guanxi'*, yet the concept and nature of the Chinese *guanxi* is still not clear, because it has various related meanings in Chinese society (Bian Y, 1994).

Meaning

This Chinese phrase "guan-xi" consists of two characters. The character "guan" means a gate or a hurdle, and "xi" refers to a tie, a relationship, or a connection, meaning "pass the gate and get connected" (Lee and Dawes, 2005). Literally, this Chinese term means "connections," "relations" or "relationships" (Chen *et al.*, 2004). In the managerial context, *guanxi* ties refer to senior managers' boundary-spanning activities and interpersonal connections, with other actors in their task environments. Senior managers are regarded as insiders of the *guanxi* networks and can enjoy the benefits that the networks beget (Chengli Shu *et al.*).

To understand *guanxi* in terms of business perspective, we may refer to a study conducted by Lee and Dawes (2005). On the basis of interviews of five sales managers from a Hong Kong company, and a dozen sales managers in China, they stated the essence of *guanxi* as "it is just like door steps. If you're not yet on the steps, no one will do business with you. If we don't know you, how can we trust you! Once you're on the door steps, then we started to know you, then we open the door to talk business with you." This is unlike the United States, in which strangers can immediately begin talking business, after they are introduced by a third person.

Nature and Dimensions

Unlike popular belief, *guanxi* is not unique to China, business in Japan, Korea and India is permeated by similar thinking, as are, to a large extent, cultures worldwide (Ambler, 1994) but, Chinese *guanxi* is distinct in terms of attributes (nature). Lee and Dawes (2005) arrived at three important characteristics of *guanxi*, namely, (i) it is a formality, (ii) there is a threshold level below which strangers remain strangers, and (iii) its establishment may take time. Hwang (1987) categorized *guanxi* into three levels of social connection: expressive ties (apply to family members and close relatives), mixed ties (apply to neighbours and friends) and instrumental ties. Instrumental ties refer to personal relationships that serve only as a means to attain other objectives (Wong *et al.*, 2007). Figure 1 shows the dimensions of *guanxi* as given by them.

Figure 1 shows the three dimensions and their components. Face or *Mianzi* is the major component of expressive ties. Commitment is the focus of the instrumental ties. Mixed ties are the relationships involving both expressive and instrumental components (as shown by arrows in the figure). Face to favour exchange, continuity, cooperation leading to commitment explain the dynamics of *guanxi*.

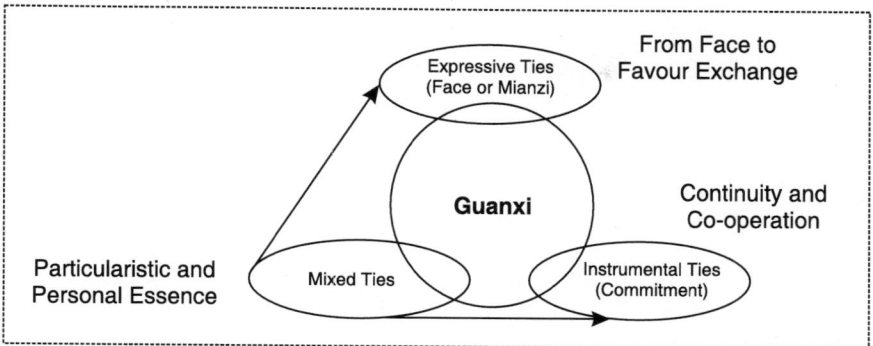

Fig. 1

Dunning and Kim (2007) have also listed the various attributes (traits) of *guanxi* as shown in a study by Luo (2000). Table 1 lists the attributes.

Table 1

Utilitarian	Guanxi is purposefully driven by personal interests.
Reciprocal	An individual's reputation is tied up with reciprocal obligations.
Transferable	Guanxi is transferable through a third party as a referral.
Personal	Guanxi is established between individuals.
Long Term	Guanxi is reinforced through long-term cultivation.
Intangible	Guanxi is maintained by an unspoken commitment.

Source: John H. Dunning and Changsu Kim "The Cultural Roots of Guanxi: An Exploratory Study", The World Economy, 2007.

Managerial Perspectives of Guanxi: Earlier Studies

Many authors have attempted to study business/managerial perspectives of *guanxi*. This section reviews some of the prominent work in this area.

Wong *et al.* (2007) proposed an unique perspective which is particularly useful when buyer and seller interact with each other with different conflicting perceptions, expectations and experience. Their conceptual framework helps businessmen to restructure their portfolios of CRM strategies, so they can enhance their CRM programs efficiently and effectively.

Braendle *et al.* (2005) analyzed the influence of *guanxi* on the Chinese corporate governance system. They found that *guanxi* is in general, a double-edged sword, but business-to-government (B2G) *guanxi* in particular, can harm the weak Chinese corporate governance system, and hamper its further economic development and growth. B2G *guanxi* does indeed have the power to even weaken the corporate governance system further, and therefore harm China in its economic competition with other countries, and hinder its economic growth potential.

Carlisle and Flynn (2005) extended the work of Tsang, Luo, Peng and others to describe the concept of *guanxi* as a means of garnering social capital, in order to maintain legitimacy (for private enterprises, state enterprises and joint venture firms). They suggested the *guanxi* construct as a strategy for entrepreneurs to further their attempts, at achieving legitimacy through threshold of legitimacy.

Wattie and Everette (2001) showed that although *guanxi* networking is necessary, it is not sufficient for minimizing legal uncertainties. *Guanxi* building can protect foreigners from trouble in a gray legal environment, and a joint venture strategy can facilitate *guanxi* building.

Wong and Tjosvold (2010) collected data from 100 paired competitors operating in Shanghai, China. Using the structural equation analysis, they showed that a high level of *guanxi* reduces the competitive approach to conflict, that in turn results in partnership effectiveness. This provides the foundation for effective collaboration between competitors in China, and perhaps in other countries as well.

Chen *et al.* (2004) conducted two studies to examine the effect of *guanxi* practices in human resource management. The first study found a negative effect of *guanxi* practices on trust in management. The second study showed that the negative effect of *guanxi* practices varied as a function of *guanxi* bases (favouring a nephew or a hometown fellow lowered trust, but favouring a college schoolmate or a close friend did not).

Chang and Peirchyi (2005) studied the relationship between managers' initiative towards a *guanxian* formation, and their transactional decisions within the network. Results showed that managers' initiative in setting up a *guanxi* network has an important impact on their perceptions towards members in the network; and in turn, the perception has an impact on their transactional decisions within the *guanxi* network. Katherine and Pearce (1996) conducted a study based on interviews that compared to the other executives, private-company executives considered business connections more important, depended more on connections for protection, had more government connections, gave more unreciprocated gifts, and trusted their connections more.

Guanxi as a Competitive Advantage Strategy

This section discusses the managerial implications of *guanxi* for organizational success.

By generating flexibility and favours, a well established *guanxi* can provide rich benefits for managers. Strong *guanxi* leads to high degree of satisfaction in a business relationship. It also prevents competitors from opportunistic behavior. A *guanxi* network, through commitments to return favours, tends to minimize the risk of uncertainty. Also, *guanxi* as a strategy can be used as an instrument at shaping core competencies, and integrating capabilities into organizational context.

The managerial application of *guanxi* can be viewed from Michael E. Porter's *Value Chain Analysis* perspective shown in Exhibit I. Porter's value chain consists of nine generic categories of value activities. Value is measured by the amount that buyers are willing to pay for a product or service. Profit margin is the excess between value and the cost of performing the value activities.

Exhibit I: The Value Chain

Support activity	Firm infrastructure					
	Human resource management					
	Technology development					
	Procurement					
	Inbound logistics	Operations	Outbound logistics	Marketing and sales	Service	
	Primary activities					**Margin**

Source: Michael E. Porter and Victor E. Millar, "How Information gives you competitive advantage", *Harvard Business Review*, July–August 1985, 149–174.

Exhibit II: The Value System

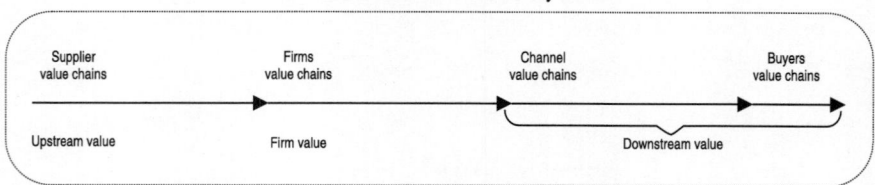

Supplier value chains	Firms value chains	Channel value chains	Buyers value chains
Upstream value	Firm value	Downstream value	

Source: Michael E. Porter and Victor E. Millar, "How Information gives you competitive advantage", *Harvard Business Review*, July–August 1985, 149–174.

Exhibit II describes how the different value chains are inter-linked. It is very essential that these linkages are carefully managed for gaining competitive advantage in the market. *Guanxi* can play an important role here.

Each value activity reflects the collective cost of performing all its value activities relative to rivals. Through *guanxi*, two business units may share one sales force to sell their products, or the units may coordinate the procurement of common components, thus yielding competitive advantage over rivals.

It can be seen in Exhibit II that the supplier value chains and buyer value chains are interconnected, with firm value chain and channel value chain. *guanxi* or interpersonal relations, can be used to strengthen the supplier and channel value chains. Using *guanxi*, long term supplier relations can be created. To illustrate in terms of suppliers, if firm A wishes to have a cost advantage, it can get a favour from the supplier regarding timely delivery, discounts and credit. If A does not have *guanxi* with the supplier, but can find someone (X) from his *guanxi* network who has a *guanxi* with the supplier, then A can ask X for an introduction to the supplier. Once the *guanxi* is established between A and the supplier, favours can be exchanged, such as favourable credit terms, extended payment periods, assured supplies, etc. all resulting in competitive advantage.

Sales growth can be achieved through favours in repayments. Using the *guanxian* network, the firm's value can be enhanced in the initial stages by getting difficult sales contracts. As far as the buyer value chain is concerned, firms reliant on personal selling can benefit from strong *guanxi* connections. The value activities function in a dynamic and uncertain environment. *Guanxi* relationships can help firms keep abreast of changes in government policies, changes in government conditions for getting licenses and permits. Thus, a strong *guanxi* network can be used in the value chain system to generate profit margins.

Many leading multinationals like Xerox, Motorola and Wal-Mart have gained from their *guanxian* networks in the Chinese markets. Xerox could achieve market leadership in China through its dealer *guanxian* network. Motorola expanded its market in China by upholding its face (commitment). Wal-Mart's entry into China has its foundations in *guanxi*.

Conclusion

Guanxi based business practices with governments, competitors, dealers, competitors and customers should be recognized as a competitive advantage strategy. Many leading companies have benefitted from it in China. However, *guanxi* has a dark side too. It can jeopardize the very existence of a firm, because of over-burdening of corporate obligations and network failures. The firms that appropriately apply this strategy can enhance their chances of success in China.

Acknowledgements

I wish to acknowledge and thank the FORE School of Management for giving me an opportunity to understand Chinese culture, business practices during the FDP 2011, China. This visit helped me to understand various aspects of China in an enjoyable manner. It is during this visit that I was introduced to the concept of Guanxi. The concept and its mechanism interested me and resulted in this piece of work. My work in this area is still in its initial stages, but I wish to explore it further in future.

References

Ambler Tim, "Marketing's Third Paradigm: Guanxi", *Business Strategy Review*, Vol. 5, No. 4, winter 1994, 69–80.

Bian, Y, "Work and Ineuity in Urban China", *Albany: State University of New York Press*, 1994.

Braendle Udo C., Tanja Gasser and Juergen Noll, "Corporate Governance in China—Is Economic Growth Potential Hindered by Guanxi?", *Business and Society Review*, 110(4), 2005, 389–405.

Carlisle Elliot and Dave Flynn, "Small Business Survival In China: Guanxi, Legitimacy and Social Capital", *Journal of Developmental Entrepreneurship*, Vol. 10, No. 1, 2005, 79–96.

Chang William Li and Peirchyi Lii, "The impact of Guanxi on Chinese managers' transactional decisions: A study of Taiwanese SMEs", *Human Systems Management*, 24, 2005, 215–222.

Chen Chao C., Ya-Ru Chen and Katherine Xin, "Guanxi Practices and Trust in Management: A Procedural Justice Perspective", *Organization Science*, Vol. 15, No. 2, March–April 2004, 200–209.

Dunning John H. and Changsu Kim, "The Cultural Roots of Guanxi: An Exploratory Study", *The World Economy*, 2007, 329–341.

Gu Flora F., Kineta Hung and David K. Tse, "When Does Guanxi Matter? Issues of Capitalization and Its Dark Sides", *Journal of Marketing*, Vol. 72, July 2008, 12–28.

Hwang K.K., "Face and Favour: The Chinese Power Game", *American Journal of Sociology*, 92, 1987, 944–974.

Lee Don Y. and Philip L. Dawes, "Guanxi, Trust, and Long-Term Orientation in Chinese Business Markets", *Journal of International Marketing*, Vol. 13, No. 2, 2005, 28–56.

Lo Wattie C.W. and Andre' M. Everette, "Thriving in the Regulatory Envronment of E-Commerce in China: A Guanxi Strategy", *Sam Advanced Management Journal*, summer 2001, 17–24.

Luo, Y., Guanxi and Business (Singapore: World Scientific), 2000.

Porter Michael E. and Victor E. Millar, "How Information gives you Competitive Advantage", *Harvard Business Review*, July–August 1985, 149–174.

Shu Chengli, Shangxing Gao, Xu Jiang and Albert L. Page, "Managerial Guanxi Ties, Knowledge Creation, and Firm Innovation: Evidence from China", *Academy of Management Annual Meeting Proceedings is the property of Academy of Management*.

Wong Y.H., T.K.P. Leung, Humphry Hung and E.W.T. Ngai, "A Model of Guanxi Development: Flexibility, Commitment and Capital Exchange", *Total Quality Management*, Vol. 18, No. 8, October 2007, 875–887.

Wong Yui-Tim, Shiu-Ho Wong and Yui-Woon Wong, "A study of subordinate–supervisor guanxi in Chinese joint ventures", *The International Journal of Human Resource Management*, Vol. 21, No. 12, October 2010, 2142–2155.

Wong, Alfred and Dean Tjosvold, "Guanxi and Conflict Management for Effective Partnering with Competitors in China", *British Journal of Management*, Vol. 21, 2010, 772–788.

Xin Katherine R. and Jone L. Pearce, "Guanxi: Connections as Substitutes for Formal Institutional Support", *Academy of Management Journal*, 1996, Vol. 39, No. B, 1641–1658.

Changing Conflict Handling Styles with Variations in Chinese Cultural Orientations

Prachi Bhatt

FORE School of Management, New Delhi

E-mail: prachi@fsm.ac.in

ABSTRACT

Impacted by changes in the socio-economic environment, cultures evolve over time. Changes in cultural constituents lead to cultural transformations. Like any other culture, changes in Chinese cultural-mix are also evident by virtue of economic development and social modernisation. The article highlights the blend of changes impacting alteration in the distinct Chinese culture, and consequently different patterns of conflict handling styles. The article attempts to focus on the need to get hold of evidence and understand underpinning factors governing contemporary Chinese styles of conflict handling and their use as against traditional styles.

Keywords: Culture, Cultural Changes, Chinese Culture, Conflict Handling Styles.

Culture

Culture can develop through recurrent social relationships, forming patterns that are eventually internalized by members of the entire group. It can be learned, interrelated and shared Hall (1977) as cited in Spangle and Isenhart (2003). There are convincing demonstrations that culture has a bearing on the conflict handling styles of people. Being a deep-rooted aspect of a person's life, one cannot manage to avoid his or her cultural assumptions, images, prejudices and behavioral traits, while resolving conflicting situations.

Chinese culture has always intrigued researchers, a culture that has drawn its roots from Confucianism. Confucianism is not exactly a religion, but distinctive values i.e. respect and love for fellow Chinese, and is primarily concerned with social orders and governance (Ma, 2011). Confucianism has had quiet an influence on Chinese management styles, inclusive of conflict handling and negotiation styles (Ma, 2011). Cultures do change. This philosophy has got more support over the years, rather than the viewpoint of persistence of the culture. As we know, that culture includes learned behaviour and values that are transmitted through shared experience, are continuously evolved through constant embellishment and adaptation. Chinese culture is also being impacted by these adaptations, by virtue of external and internal environmental forces of change.

Change in the Chinese Cultural Make-up

However, the degree of cultural changes may vary across national or regional boundaries of cultures; transformation can be attributed to the changes in elements of cultural like: communication patterns, importance given to teams/individuals, relationships and inter-dependence orientation, tolerance to uncertainty, long or short term orientations, perception about power, significance given to terminal or instrumental values, etc. According to Wilkins and Patterson (1985) as cited in Kilman *et al.* (1985), culture can be explained as it is 'like a person's character or personality and is, therefore, changed through processes of growth, rather than through engineering.' Chinese culture also has undergone a blend of changes in cultural elements that seem to have complicated the understanding of the distinct Chinese culture and conflict handling strategies.

The very definition of culture is the source of convergence or crossvergence of culture; of which a person and the society are originally a part. In today's world of an integrated world economy, cultures have become increasingly prone to different social and commercial cultures. Just like any other culture, traditional Chinese culture is also exposed to various influencers like, rapid political, economic, and social changes. Opportunities to get exposed to other cultures, underlying values and its benefits (also their drawbacks) abet transformation. Facilitated by technology, exposure to 'other' culture, its values, lifestyles and business styles has been found to have impacted Chinese culture. The cultural identity of an individual is subjected to variations and so are an individual's values, moral and ethical viewpoints, theological beliefs, norms, etc. and their interpretation, which itself is subjected to variations, especially in today's context. Norms play an influential role in controlling a culture and norms can be surfaced, discussed, and altered (Kilmann *et al.*, 1985). This resulted changes in Chinese culture, in both content and strength of culture, although gradual.

Main factors that originally used to influence Chinese conflict resolution strategies are: harmony, network (*guanxi*), face (*miantze*), holistic thinking, power distance/hierarchy, in-group/out-group, ideology of extended family and group, high contextualism, long-term orientation. Changes in the cultural constituents affect the styles of conflict handling approaches of the Chinese. Also, three other important dimensions of culture i.e. cultural context, difference in the language, and thinking patterns that affect conflict management or resolution strategies to a great extent (Chen and Starosta, 1997–8). Alterations in the social and economic behaviour of the Chinese people like in conflicting situations, have been observed (not empirically) but are slow.

Change in these aspects; invite an understanding of their implications on Chinese conflict managing strategies. There is no linear path to cultural change. Exposure to different cross-border geographies, international practices and different languages (an important part of a culture), etiquettes, interpersonal relationship protocols, different socio-economic codes have the essence for influencing the means and the processes of conflict resolution. Also, change in priorities, evaluative attitudes, thinking patterns, and decision-making processes, by virtue of cultural transformation, substantially affect the strategy and style to manage conflicts and negotiations of the Chinese. Awareness about the new has given Chinese counterparts the opportunity to have knowledge of other styles and tactics at their disposal, to be used in their favour while managing conflicting situations.

Demographic attributes like-improving education levels and changing gender roles; and intergenerational population replacement cannot be ignored, while attempting to realise changes. Alterations seem to have their influence over the manner a Chinese person sees his culture and applications of the same, like, styles of conflict management, negotiations that are brought into play and manipulated. While studying Chinese conflict management and resolution, it is especially important to examine the influence of Chinese wisdom other than Confucianism, like Taoism.

Summary and Conclusion

The culture that we see is the version of a culture that has evolved over the indigenous one. So it's also important to understand the significance of the offshoots of a culture, as a result of change. Social modernaisation has led to alterations in Chinese culture. Also, it has been observed that economic development is related with widespread cultural changes, and that it also predicts changes in the same to a certain degree (Inglehart and Baker, 2000). With economic development, social modernization can be simultaneous or an after-effect. Researchers have found changes in the psychology and personality of the Chinese, their values, needs, orientation towards achievement, individualistic orientations, and traditional values of self-contentment (Yang, 1996).

Cultural changes have resulted in growing indistinctiveness in 'Chinese' business styles, or may be the emergence of different patterns. Chinese culture is directed towards change, but, possibly not crossvergence or convergence into another culture, as there is no such evidences to prove this. Nevertheless, the existence and influence of different patterns mushrooming in Chinese culture cannot be disregarded.

It would be interesting to know whether and to what extent the traditional culture and values are still prevalent in contemporary Chinese approaches to handle conflicts. Also, evidence of how change in priorities, evaluative attitudes, thinking patterns, and decision-making processes may help to gauge the range of Chinese styles of resolving conflicts and their applications.

Although, Confucianism acts as the backbone of Chinese culture, variations within the culture can be attributed to other ancient wisdom i.e. Taoism, Buddhism, and Legalism which seem to have contributed to Chinese styles (Lu, 1994) to resolve conflicts. While assessing conflict management and resolution, it is important to trace the contributions of other philosophies, separately or collaboratively, on Chinese conflict behaviours, particularly strategies to resolve conflicts.

Other schools of thought believe in an enduring and persistent nature of a culture. As there have been philosophies with strong support for changing culture, the knowledge of various styles of managing conflict is at the disposal of Chinese counterpart. As to what motives and in what conditions and why do Chinese retain their traditional styles of conflict management? And why do they adopt new styles? Evidence with respect to these questions may yield useful information. This can be looked into for the overseas Chinese as well, as Chinese visas (or visa of PRC) does not guarantee the assumptions and styles of handling issues while in conflict situations, in negotiations and other management styles. The underpinning factors contemporary Chinese styles of managing, conflict handling and negotiations are not yet clear. Thus, leaves us with areas to be explored about Chinese culture and other cultures as well.

References

Chen, G.M. and Starosta, W.J. (1998). 'Chinese Conflict Management and Resolution: Overview and Implications', *Intercultural Communication Studies*, Vol. 7, No. 1, pp. 1–13.

Fang, T. (1999) *Chinese Business Negotiation Style*, Thousand Oaks, CA: Sage Publications, pp. 109.

Inglehart, R. and Baker, W.E. (2000) 'Modernization, Cultural Change, and the Persistence of Traditional Values', *American Sociological Review*, Vol. 65, No. 1, pp. 19–51.

Kilman, R.H., Saxton, M.J. and Serpa, R. (1985). *Gaining control of the corporate culture*, San Francisco: Jossey-Bass, pp. 262–291.

Lu, X. (1994). 'Theory of persuasion in Han Fei Tzu and its impact on chinese communication behavior', *The Howard Journal of Communications*, Vol. 5, pp. 108–122.

Ma, Z. (2011). *Some Thoughts about Chinese Management Styles and Chinese Business Ethics*, Faculty Development Program organized by FORE School of Management, 29 October–01 November. Beijing, China.

Spangle, M.L. and Isenhart, M.W. (2003). *Negotiation: Communication for diverse settings*, Thousand Oaks, California: Sage Publications.

Yang, K.S. (1996). 'The psychological transformation of Chinese people as a result of societal modernization', in Bond, M.H. (ed.), *The handbook of Chinese psychology* Hong Kong: Oxford University Press, pp. 479–498.

A Critique on the Chinese Management Style and Business Ethics: Lessons for Hindustani Business

Ambrish Gupta

FORE School of Management, New Delhi

E-mail: ambrish@fsm.ac.in

ABSTRACT

This article seeks to carry out a critical analysis of the Chinese management style and business ethics as learnt from a seminar on *"Some Thoughts about Chinese Management Styles and Chinese Business Ethics"*, delivered by Professor Zhenzhong Ma in Beijing, China, on 01 November, 2011. The article further seeks to suggest lessons for Hindustani businessmen while dealing with their Chinese counterparts.

Keywords: Confucianism, Chinese Management Style, Chinese Business Ethics, Gender Effects.

Introduction

The FORE School of Management, sponsored a faculty visit to China between 28/29 October 2011 to 2 November 2011 and organised a Faculty Development Seminar at Beijing on October 31 and November 1 with the broad objective of *'International Exposure to FORE Faculty'* with inputs on the local business scenario, including interacting with Chinese people in an informal setting. The seminar had four sessions including the one on *"Some*

Thoughts about Chinese Management Styles and Chinese Business Ethics" by Professor Zhenzhong Ma, a Chinese professor teaching at the University of Windsor, Ontario, Canada. His presentation was set in the backdrop of Chinese culture, which according to him, owes its origin and development to Confucianism, and its impact on Chinese management styles and business ethics. The subject evoked great interest among the faculty members and the much skilled oratory of the young professor added further flavour to the detailed and lengthy presentation which made the session a very interactive one.

Objectives

The author intends to present some of his views on what he learnt and understood during this session of the seminar. This understanding suggests that there is a lot that Hindustani businessmen can learn, to be able to score over their Chinese counterparts, or at least to save their interests and be in a position to present avoidable losses while dealing with them. The specific objectives behind this article are as follows:

- To carry out an analysis of the Chinese management styles and business ethics as learnt from the seminar.
- To further disseminate this learning and analysis and share it with a larger audience.
- To suggest lessons for Hindustani businessmen while dealing with their Chinese counterparts.

Towards the fulfillment of these objectives, the author now proceeds to provide a synoptic view of the comprehensive presentation of Professor Zhenzhong Ma, and his observations thereon coupled, simultaneously, with a discussion and analysis and his personal experience of the Chinese dictum that '*too much respect is better than inconsiderate treatment*' in Beijing, and the lessons that Hindustani business need to learn.

A Synoptic View of the Presentation

The presentation was divided into two sections:

Chinese Management Styles

The section lays down the conceptual premises and cultural factors, deeply rooted in Confucianism that have influenced Chinese management styles.

Business Ethics in China

This section presents two research studies and their outcomes:

- '*A Three-Cultural Comparison of the Perceived Ethicality of Negotiation Strategies in Business Negotiations*'. The study tests some of these factors on the Chinese, Taiwanese and Canadian business negotiators, together with gender effects on them.

- '*Ethicality vs. Practicality: Chinese Students' Cheating in the Classroom and their Propensity to Cheat in the Real Business World*'. This study seeks to explore Chinese business students' attitudes towards adopting unethical practices in the real business world, in the background of their rampant cheating in the classrooms. The research seeks to provide a futuristic view of Chinese business ethics.

Observations, Discussion and Analysis

Let us now discuss and analyze both these sections in detail, individually.

Chinese Management Styles

According to Professor Zhenzhong, these styles are based on the following cultural factors:

- *Guanxi Network:* That is relationship building. It reflects an individual's social network and social capital. A great deal of emphasis is laid on this principle. So much so that "*No Guanxi, No business*" (*And then exploit the relations to the hilt*).

- *Facework:* Or face-saving. The Chinese have been brought up to mask their feelings, often by smiling or laughing, when they confront an embarrassing situation, to avoid loss of self-respect or prestige. They prefer to say '*later*' than '*no*', often knowing well that '*later*' may never happen (*They are highly evasive*).

- *Power Distance and Hierarchy:* Highly rigid about following the hierarchy and respecting power and authority (*Wisdom of the boss is unquestionable*). So much so that '*Pretending to show too much respect is better than inconsiderate treatment*'.

- *Holistic Thinking:* Focus on principal targets. Willing to leave the negotiation table for further maneuvering, rather than presenting fixed, clear-cut plans. Flexibility in methods/strategies (*End justifies the means*).

- *Extended Family and Group:* Large joint families living under one roof. (*Unity is the best policy*). The oldest member is considered to be supreme with unqualified respect for him/her. The same philosophy extends to business also, i.e., *follow the CEO blindly*.

- *In-group Favouritism vs. Out-group:* In-group means a group of followers/individuals with the same opinion/those who fall in line. Rampant in-group favouritism is prevalent. Out-group means group of individuals with opposite opinion/who do not fall in line, and therefore are considered as enemies. Destroy them if they cannot unite with you. Be ruthless. (*Or, don't let them unite with anyone else, so as to be able to destroy them easily*).

- *High Contextualism:* Explicit language binds. Therefore, use of implicit language to the hilt. Meaning (interpretation) of the communication changes according to the needs. A contract may not be honoured if it does not suit the person/organization if the situation changes, before it has been finally executed. (*No regard for one's own words. Self-interest is supreme*). As noted earlier, it is the end that matters, not the means.

- *Long-term Orientation:* Do make sacrifices in the present. *Invest and save for the future,* rather than spend and waste today for physical pleasures, at the cost of the future which is uncertain. (*Build up hedges, shields and buffers or, in other words, a strong backup to fall upon during days of distress*).

The overall picture that emerges is that Chinese management styles and business practices are guided solely by self interest and target-orientation, with little or no regard for the ethicality of the means, and therefore they are used in adopting highly implicit communication, both written as well as verbal, since they are highly evasive too. They are never in a hurry and change their stand according to their convenience. They are ruthless towards their opponents, while pursuing their self-interest.

Professor Zhenzhong referred to Confucianism and emphasized that the Chinese attitude to life and management styles discussed earlier, is influenced by Confucian ethics, values and governance systems which are very distinctive for their *worldly emphasis* on society and wide diffusion throughout Chinese society. Thus, the Chinese style of management and governance is a fall-out of *the Confucian legacy.*

(*Note:* Opinions shown in brackets above are the author's own and personal. These have been framed on the basis of the discussions and interactions during the presentation. Professor Zhenzhong is not concerned with these opinions).

Business Ethics in China

The discussion on Chinese management styles provides enough indications of the state of the likely unethical/ethical practices of Chinese businesses. Prima facie perception that emerges is definitely short on optimism. In this section, as a test of the prevalent practical impact of the cultural factors, and likely state of ethical business practices in future, Professor Zhenzhong presented two research studies carried out by him and their outcome as mentioned earlier. A discussion and analysis of the two now follows.

'*A Three-Cultural Comparison of the Perceived Ethicality of Negotiation Strategies in Business Negotiations'* covering China, Taiwan and Canada. He picked two factors, that is, *In-Group Favouritism* and *Cultural Contextualism* to assess their *impact on the unethicality or otherwise* of business negotiation strategies, and expanded the study further to assess the related **gender effects** on such practices.

China, as noted earlier, is a *high in-group favouritism* and *high cultural contextualism country.* As per Professor Zhenzhong, *Taiwan* is a country with *high in-group favouritism* but *moderate level of cultural contextualism* and *Canada* is a *low in-group favouritism* and *low cultural contextualism* country. No explanation was provided as to why only two factors were tested. He also restricted the study to business negotiations, instead of the entire gamut of business. Negotiations are however at the heart of every business activity and present an ideal business area to test ethicality of the business negotiators. Covering the entire gamut of business activities, and the impact of all the factors might require a very large study. Professor Zhenzhong, being a Chinese professor teaching at a Canadian university, and Canada being a low in-group favouritism and low cultural contextualism country, comparison of China with Canada becomes the obvious choice for him.

The research was conducted on 619 business students consisting of 170 from China (male/female 46/54 percent), 191 from Taiwan (male/female 51/49 percent) and 258 from Canada (male/female 56/44 percent). Ideally, keeping in view the size of the three countries, the maximum number of students should have been from China, followed by Canada and

Taiwan in that order. Uniform male/female ratio would have been a better option.

Main findings of the study are as follows:

– Chinese negotiators from both mainland China and Taiwan *consider ethically questionable negotiation strategies* such as false promises, misrepresentation, inappropriate information gathering, and attacking opponent's network *as more appropriate* than Canadian negotiators, *irrespective of gender* due to prominent in-group favouritism in China and Taiwan. Thus *Chinese* are *more unethical* than *Canadians*.

– Within Canadians male negotiators consider it more appropriate to use ethically questionable negotiation strategies than female negotiators. *Canadian women* are thus *less unethical* compared to their *male counterparts*.

– In China, there are hardly any *gender differences* in the appropriateness of use of ethically questionable negotiation strategies in business negotiations. *Chinese women* are thus *more or less as unethical* as their men counterparts.

The findings of the study thus clearly support the conceptual premise that rampant in-group favouritism and high contextualism deeply embedded in the Chinese culture, have led Chinese business negotiators, *be men or women*, adopt much more unethical negotiation strategies, than their moderate/less in-group favouritism and contextualism counterparts in other parts of the globe. For them it is '*by hook or by crook*'.

• '*Ethicality vs. Practicality: Chinese Students' Cheating in the Classroom and Their Propensity to Cheat in the Real Business World*'. The research probably seeks to provide a *futuristic view* of the comparative prevalence of unethical business practices in Chinese businesses once the Chinese youth of today take command of businesses tomorrow. The research tries to link the youth's value orientation towards success in their careers *in the backdrop of their antecedents.*

Classroom cheating has been taken as the antecedent here. The study covered 205 business students comprising 44.3 percent male and 55.7 percent female representing mean—age: 24, GPA: 2.28 and grade level: 4.74.

Main findings of the study are as follows:

- A very high *77.8 percent* of Chinese business students cheat in the class *without any feelings of guilt* even though they have a *good understanding* of what constitutes ethical behaviour and the need for such behaviour.
- But self-interest being supreme, they *prefer practicality* (read: cheating/unethicality) *over ethicality* in the classroom. High scores have to be achieved in the examination, no matter even if by unfair means.
- Surprisingly, in contrast, in the *real business world* they *intend* to prefer *ethicality over practicality.*
- They believe that Chinese businessmen fail to act in an ethical manner, yet they are *unwilling* to compromise their ethical standards in order to get ahead in their future careers *except when they have a strong need for competitive success.*

Findings of this study are contradictory. Habitual practitioners of unfair practices in examinations, obviously with the objective of getting better jobs in business, better than what they deserve on the parameters of capability, are showing their *intention* and *willingness* to adopt fair practices in business, the very business where they entered through unfair means. *Does it sound convincing? Certainly not* Furthermore, they have themselves *subjected their intent and willingness* to their career advancement *needs.*

It appears that the opening of doors of business for outsiders, particularly the western world, is slowly bringing fresh air to the otherwise closed Chinese society and culture. However, '*supposed to be business leaders of tomorrow*', in China, seem to be finding themselves at the crossroads. Not sure what they really want to stick to. After all, cultural transformation takes longer than a long time. One can only wish that the future scenario of business negotiations with the Chinese and doing business with them in general should *bring some hope* of their following lesser unethical practices. Winds of change need to blow fast, however.

Pretending to Show Too Much Respect is Better than Inconsiderate Treatment

The author wishes to narrate of us an incident that happened with him in Beijing. A group of four of us hired a taxi from our hotel to a market. On reaching there, the taxi driver charged 20 yuans as per the meter. While returning back, it was around 11 PM. We were looking for a taxi and spotted a large number of them lined up on the roadside ahead. We approached one of them. The driver refused to go by the meter. Instead, to our surprise, he demanded 80 yuans, i.e., 20 yuans per person. We refused and moved over to another taxi. The same situation arose there as well. We tried five-six taxis but they all had formed a cartel. Finally, the author tried to defeat them at their own game. And took one of them a little aside and said "Why you don't ask for 1000 yuans, I will pay you that much, but not a meager 80". Now it was his turn to get surprised. His eyes first scanned the author from north to south, then south to north, and then he looked into his eyes very deeply. The trick worked and he offered to reduce his charge by 10 Yuans to 70. But that was not acceptable to the author. Who now offered him 2000 yuans. The same reaction again and the demand now declined to 60 yuans.

The author could not further bring down the rate and settled it at 60. It the author think '*pretending to be too much respectful to the driver proved to be a better strategy than inconsiderate treatment'.* After all, he had all the power and authority at that time (for that matter every taxi driver) knowing full well that we were strangers in his city and helpless, as it was already 11.30 PM then with scant traffic on the road coupled with our inability to speak the Chinese language *(The author negotiated with the help of his body language and driver's calculator).*

It happened on 31 October which the author shared with Professor Zhenzhong the next day during his session, in support of his statement that *too much respect is better than inconsiderate treatment* as per the Chinese culture and value system.

A *good firsthand experience and lesson* on negotiating with a Chinese businessman on the street in the land of the dragon: try to defeat them at their own game.

Lessons for Hindustani Business

Having analysed the TRAITS of the Chinese people, their culture, present day Chinese management styles and unethical business practices, the likely continuity of unethical practices in the future as well as, proven research by a Chinese professor himself on these issues and having personally experienced a negotiation, the author offers a few suggestions for the Hindustani business negotiators while dealing with their Chinese counterparts:

- While negotiating with the Chinese, be as careful and alert as possible. Don't forget that you are dealing with evasive people. They try to save face rather than giving in. Never take them at their face value.
- For them, end justifies the means. And therefore they can go to any extent to change their stand, again and again. Therefore, be ready for unduly long negotiations, frequent incomplete meeting sessions, and exercise extreme patience so as to make them fall in line.

- Their interpretation and reinterpretation of a single word, being highly contextual, may turn the tide, lead to disaster and convert the seemingly sure win of yours into a big loss. Be as explicit with them, and try to make them as committal through your communication skills, both verbal and written, as possible, so that the scope for multiple/alternate interpretations is minimized, if not eliminated. Read their drafts with magnifying glasses and learn to read in between the lines.

- At the same time, learn the art of high contextualism. Depending on the need and circumstances, use as flexible a language as they do. If you can't bind them, make sure that they also don't succeed in binding you.

- Prefer to *pretend* to show too much respect to them than inconsiderate treatment. Or, keep them in good humour. First inflate them. It will be easier then to puncture.

- Don't forget that you are the 'out-group' for them. Treat them also as 'out-group'. Make them fall in line, or destroy them before they destroy you. That is, be ruthless to competition. Acquire their business if you cannot beat them. Grow inorganically, if it is not possible organically.

- If the Chinese team is being led by a woman, don't expect her to be more ethical and committal than her male counterpart. This mistake may prove very costly.

- Positive relationships (*Guanxi*) that they build are meant to serve their purpose. Once the purpose is served, the relationship may become a thing of past. Keep this in mind.

- The future also does not seem to be hopeful of suggesting adoption of ethical practices by the young Chinese generation. This message needs to be percolated down to the young members of business families and young business executives of Hindustan.

- Don't forget that they invest and save for the future, or in other words, they build up a strong backup to fall upon during days of distress. This is a virtue which helps them leverage the negotiations to their advantage. This is a great strength of the Chinese businessmen. Fortunately, this strength is highly embedded in the Hindustani culture and business too. So, prefer the long term objective over the short term.

Hindustani business needs to learn and act accordingly. One more virtue of the Chinese, i.e., extended family and group living under one roof, and the same philosophy extending to business houses as well as noted earlier, which also used to be strongly embedded in Hindustani families and business houses for thousands of years, but now being disregarded gradually, teaches us to revisit our own cultural values. The message for Hindustani business houses is clear *'better don't break away'*. Competitive growth and wealth creation for all the stakeholders will be much faster and economical then. The latest case of exploring reunion by the Ambani brothers emphasizes the need to follow this philosophy the most.

Conclusion

This article has carried out a critical analysis of Chinese Management Style and Business Ethics as learnt through the seminar on "Some Thoughts about Chinese Management Styles and Chinese Business Ethics", delivered by Professor Zhenzhong Ma in Beijing, China, on November 01, 2011. The contribution of this paper lies suggesting appropriate lessons for Hindustani businessman, to succeed in negotiations, while dealing with their Chinese counterparts in the background of the learning from the said seminar.

Acknowledgements

My sincere thanks and gratitude to the President, FORE, Shri R.C. Sharma, for providing an opportunity to the FORE faculty to visit

China to understand its people, culture, management styles and business practices.

Reference

Zhenzhong Ma (2011). "Some Thoughts about Chinese Management Styles and Chinese Business Ethics", Presentation at seminar in Beijing, China, November 01, 2011.

Understanding the Role of Cultural Ethos in Chinese Management

Neetu Jain

FORE School of Management, New Delhi

E-mail: neetujain@fsm.ac.in

ABSTRACT

This article examines the relationship between cultural ethos and management in the People's Republic of China [PRC]. Chinese culture is a blend of Chinese traditional culture and western culture. Chinese culture is one of the world's oldest and most complex cultures. Culture has a powerful impact on management and organization behaviour. It is treated as one of the main variables accounting for specific management scenarios, that have evolved in China over the last few decades (Warner and Joynt, 2002). In a rapidly changing and varied context such as contemporary China, it is not easy to assess the degree to which traditional culture continues to exert any influence on management values and behaviour. Modern Chinese management has derived management wisdom from its deep cultural roots. This article examines the extent to which management in China will be fashioned according to international 'best practice,' as opposed to following its own principles and practices.

Keywords: Chinese Culture, Chinese Management, Cultural Ethos, HR Practices.

Introduction

This article examines the relationship between cultural ethos and management in the People's Republic of China [PRC]. Chinese culture is a blend of Chinese traditional culture and western culture. Chinese culture is one of the world's oldest and most complex cultures. Culture has a powerful impact on management and organization behaviour. It is treated as one of the main variables accounting for specific management scenarios that have evolved in China over the last few decades (Warner and Joynt, 2002). In a rapidly changing and varied context such as contemporary China, it is not easy to assess the degree to which traditional culture continues to exert any influence on management values and behaviour. China has been shaped by its history. Modern Chinese management has derived management wisdom from its deep cultural roots.

While Chinese management values and behaviour have been importantly conditioned by the country's political and economic system, Chinese culture has also had an enduring influence, and is today free of the active hostility it experienced under Maoism. The big issue has become the extent to which management in China will be fashioned according to international 'best practice,' as opposed to following its own principles and practices.

Understanding Culture

The word culture has been adopted from Latin culture which is related to cultus, cult or worship. Cult in Latin means to inhabit, till or worship and are defined as 'the result of'; thus in the broadest sense, one might define culture as 'the result of human action' (Berthon 1993). Culture is the collective programming of the mind which distinguishes members of one human group from another. (Hofstede, 1982: 21). Hall (1959) suggests that culture is the pattern taken for granted assumptions, about how a given collection of people should think, act and feel as they go about their daily affairs.National differences can simply be expressed in cultural terms, and that the nation can be used as the unit of analysis for culture (Gannon 1994). Culture therefore, differentiates management across nations and other social collectivities. The two best known cultural perspectives that have been applied to management and organizations, are those of Hofstede (1980 b: 1991) and Trompenaars (1993). A literature survey by Adler and Bartholomew (1992) supports the view that culture has a strong impact on organizational behavior and the individual behaviours of employees.

Understanding Chinese Cultural Ethos and Management

Given the external competitive pressures to adopt new forms of organization, such as teamwork (Child and McGrath 2001), it will be instructive to see whether Chinese cultural attributes help or hinder this process. As Chen *et al.* (2000) note, the collectivist orientation, importance of relationships and concern for harmony in Chinese culture, might assist crucial aspects of teamwork such as a common purpose, task interdependence and a group orientation.

Chinese managers, and perhaps people in general, are more flexible in their cultural referents than theorists such as Hofstede (1980, 1991) assume is normal for adults. Chinese people who are exposed to 'Western' values through their roles at work, or equally through their roles as consumers, may retain the option to segment their cultural mind-sets and switch between them. For instance, if conforming to certain Western norms and practices offers material attractions, such as higher pay in return for accepting individual responsibility for performance, then Chinese staff may decide to go along with them within the confines of their workplace roles. They may also be encouraged to accept practices imported from another culture, if these are perceived to be part of a more comprehensive policy, justified as 'best international practice,' offering other benefits such as equitable treatment, comprehensive training, and good prospects for advancement. This is why employment with a multinational corporation's joint venture, or subsidiary is usually highly prized by Chinese managers. At the same time, as they switch social identity in 'converting' to their non-work roles in the family and community, they could well revert to a more traditional Chinese cultural mind-set (Child and Warner 2003).

The implications of the shift from a centrally planned economy to market socialism has been considerable for managers. Translating high-level macro-economic policy into micro-economic detail is no mean task, but many key shifts have taken place. Before the early 1980s for instance, managers had very limited autonomy and could neither hire nor fire their workers. Like their employees, their performance was not linked to their efforts; motivation was low; mobility was very restricted and in many cases, non-existent. Today, all that has changed and managers have significantly expanded powers, but it did not occur at once. Over the 1980s and 1990s, China underwent a 'managerial revolution' (Warner 2000).

The enterprise and management reforms of 1984, the labour reforms of 1986, the personnel reforms of 1992 and so on, proved to be major landmarks on the 'long march' to market-driven management. After these reforms of the 1980s and 1990s promoted by Deng Xiaoping, managers found their roles had become much more market driven. But, more than strategy and structure changed; mind-sets also were radically transformed. Chinese managers became responsible for financial performance targets, and could be more significantly rewarded if they did well. Some larger formerly state-owned firms have been floated on the internal and external stock exchanges. Recently, there have even been a significant number of 'management buy-outs.'

The strong element of particularism in Chinese culture (Trompenaars, 1993) has practical significance for business transactions, in terms of who you know and the basis on which the relationship is understood to rest. This accounts for the considerable attention given to the notion of *guanxi* that captures this characteristic. It contrasts with universalism, which denotes that it is culturally appropriate to apply the same rules and standards, whoever the person may be.

Studies (e.g. Chiu *et al.* 1998) of mainland Chinese managerial values suggest that younger managers in urban coastal locations are adopting new values. This points to the impact that modernization and increased contact with the rest of the world may be having on Chinese managerial values. However, the extent to which traditional Confucian values are being diluted or forsaken, remains open to question. Whether the 'new' Chinese managers hold a combination of new and traditional values deserves further investigation, as does the possibility that such managers maintain a distinction between the values that apply to the workplace, and those they regard as appropriate to private and community life. The apparently changing nature of Chinese managerial values reflects, at the individual level, China's paradoxical struggle to compete and succeed in the modern world economy, while at the same time, maintaining social traditions (the unique 'Chinese characteristics') that have preserved the unity of the country for over 2000 years (Boisot and Child 1996).

HRM Practices in the People's Republic of China

The HRM function is probably the most culture bound function of all management functions and is therefore, more likely to resist any attempts to standardize practices across cultures, as can be seen in debates regarding its implementation in China (Warner 1995). Indeed, Edwards, Ferner and Sisson (1996) point out that a few MNEs have used global culture management techniques and HRM practices successfully to integrate their multiple affiliates. In the literature, this dilemma is also referred to as the integration-differentiation puzzle (Kamoche 1996).

An interesting idea is that different HRM practices vary with regard to their cross cultural transferability (Rosenzweig and

Nohria 1994). Furthermore, it is also the HRM function which is particularly exposed to local labour regulating laws and other local stakeholders, eg, trade unions (Rosenzweig and Nohria 1994). A cross cultural transfer of HRM philosophies, policies and practices into varying economic, politico-legal and socio-cultural contexts might not only lead to organizational inefficiencies (Kanungo and Jaeger 1990), but might also lead to a disruption of indigenous ways of organizing (Marsden, 1991). It is assumed that recruitment and training are less culture bound, because they are characterized by the technical ingredients attached to various positions (Anderson 1992, Watson 1994). A production manager,for example,needs to possess a set of skills, educational background and experiences independent of the country in which he or she performs. On the other hand, HRM practices such as promotion, P.A and financial compensation are more distinctive from one country to another, because they are induced by socio-cultural factors (Hofstede, 1982). There is some empirical evidence which supports the assumption of differences in cross cultural transferability of HRM practices.

Warner (1995) has highlighted the difficulties in applying exogenous concepts like HRM, in the Chinese context. The translation of HRM into Chinese is *renli ziyuan guanli* which means labour force resources management. Infact, some people now use it as a synonym for 'personnel management' (*renshi guanli*) and indeed treat it as such (Warner 1995). In their example of 65 Sino-Western joint ventures, Lu and Bjorkman (1997) found that recruitment and training did indeed appear to be less culture bound than promotion, PA and financial compensation. Similarly research by Chile (1994) which also focused on Sino-western joint ventures, showed that introduction of foreign approaches in appraising,promotion and career development were not very successful, whereas new approaches in payment and staffing showed somewhat higher success rates (Child etal 1994; Child 1991: 101). The former approaches can be deemed to be less successful, because they touch sensitive fields in the social and political context of Chinese enterprises, since they are functional areas where foreign approaches can be assumed to be furthest removed from the collective norms of Chinese tradition and socialist ideology (Child, 1994: 181). Easterby-Smith, Malina and Lu (1995) see the main differences in HRM between the People's Republic of China and the UK companies, because they studied in the softer functional areas where relationships matter, such as appraising practices, the assessment of management potential and reward systems (Easterby-Smith, Malina and Lu 1994:55) context.

Generation Y in China, provides unique management challenges for all companies. They are more individualistic than previous generations, more information oriented, more financial gain oriented, and more demanding than their predecessors, many of whom are now managing them. Individualism is low in Chinese employees, so motivating Chinese employees is less about money, but more about creating working conditions where people can better assure their mutual harmony and socialization needs, for example, creating a congenial working space and promoting team bonding (Zhou, 2011).

Concluding Remarks

China offers a challenging and fascinating arena for further exploration of the theoretical and practical issues associated with culture and management. The reforms of the last two decades have changed the management system from a one based on a command economy, to one more market driven and with increased private ownership. However, Chinese people are quick to maintain that these changes have been given 'Chinese characteristics,' implying that whatever the immediate institutional and organizational details, the underlying norms and values may reflect continuity as much as change. Understanding China's Gen Y 's in the context of its peers, and its unique upbringing and internal motivations, is the starting point for China's managers to develop and implement workplace best practices.

References

Adler, N.J. and Baetholomew, S. (1992). Academic and professional communities of discourse: generating knowledge on transnational HRM, Journal of international business studies, 23: 551–69.

Berthon, P.R. (1993). Psychological type and corporate cultures: relationships and dynamics, Omega 21(3): 329–44.

Boisot, M. and Child, J. (1996). From Fiefs to Clans and Network Capitalism: Explaining China's Emerging Economic Order. Administrative Science Quarterly, 41(4): 600–628.

Chen, X., Bishop, J.W. and Dow, S.K. (2000). Teamwork in China: Where Reality Challenges Theory and Practice. In J.T. Li, A.S. Tsui and E. Weldon (eds.). Management and Organizations in the Chinese Context: 269–282. Basingstoke: Macmillan.

Child, J. (1981) Culture, Contingency and Capitalism in the cross national study of organizations, in LL Cummings and B.M.Staw (eds), Research in O.B, Vol. 3, Greenwich: JAI Press.

Child, J. (1991). A foreign perspective on the management of people in China, International journal of HRM, 2: 93–107.

Child, J. (1994). Management in China during the age of reform, Cambridge: Cambridge University Press.

Child, J. and McGrath, R.G. (2001). Organizations Unfettered: Organizational Form in an Information-intensive Economy. *Academy of Management Journal*, 44 (6): 1135–1148.

Child, J. and Warner, M. (2003). Culture and Management in China, Working paper 03/2003, Cambridge, U.K.

Chiu, C.H., Ting, K., Tso, G.F.K. and He, C. (1998). A Comparison of Occupational Values between Capitalist Hong Kong and Socialist Guangzhou. Economic Development and Cultural Change, 46(3): 144–151.

Hall, E.T. (1959). The silent language, New York: Doubleday.

Hofstede, G. (1980). Cultures Consequences: International differences in work related values, Beverly Hills, CA, and London: Sage.

Joyant, P.D. and Warner, M. (1985). Managing in different cultures, Oslo: Universitetsforloget.

Kanungo, R.N. and Jaeger, A.M. (1990). Introduction: the need for indigenous management in developing countries, in AM Jaeger and R.N.Kanungo (eds.) Management in developing countries, London: Routledge.

Lu, Y. and Bjorkman, I. (1997). HRM practices in China-western joint ventures: MNC standardization versus localization, International journal of HRM 8: 614–27.

Marsden, D. (1991). Indigenous management, International journal of HRM 2: 21–38.

Rosenzweig, P.M. and Nohria, N. (1994). Influences on HRM practices in MNCs, Journal of international business studies 25: 229–51.

Trompenaars, F. (1993). Riding the Waves of Culture. London: Economist Books. Xu J. 1997. Managerial Communication within a Chinese State-Owned Enterprise in a Period of Transition. Unpublished MPhil thesis, University of Hong Kong.

Warner, M. (1995). The management of Human resources in Chinese industry, Basingstoke: Macmillan, New York: St Martin's Press.

Zhou, Gill (Oct., 2011). Collaborating with Gen Y: Leveraging generational insight to build the best workplace for Gen Y in China, NHRD Network Journal, Vol. 4, Issue 4,

NI HAO-Hello this is the Chinese Way…!

Anita Tripathy Lal

FORE School of Management, New Delhi

E-mail: anita@fsm.ac.in

ABSTRACT

At the advent of globalization, China has started to exert powerful influence in virtually every dimension of the global business. It has been predicted that in the coming decades, China along with India, are going to be the biggest forces reshaping the world economy. This article attempts to find out how the Chinese way of doing business is different from doing business globally. To understand the Chinese ways of doing business, styles of business communication, mannerisms at the workplace, meetings and negotiations have been analyzed.

Keywords: Business, Communication, Meeting, Negotiation.

Introduction

At the advent of globalization, China has started to exert a powerful influence in virtually every dimension of the global business. It has been predicted that in the coming decades, China along with India are going to be the biggest forces reshaping the world economy. India now boasts of the second highest growth rate in the world after China.

This research attempts to find out how the Chinese way of doing business is different from doing business globally. According to the famous anthropologist Edward T. Hall, people behave differently across the globe, because they primarily belong to two different groups i.e., the low context and the high context. The Americans, Australians, Europeans belong to the Low context group whereas, Asians, Africans and Arabians belong to the high context group. As China has been doing so well, it becomes imperative to examine how China has been doing business all these years. To understand the Chinese ways of doing business, the following objectives have been outlined as follows:

Objectives of the Study

1. To understand the Chinese styles of communication.
2. To examine the Chinese mannerisms at workplace.
3. To assess the Chinese ways of conducting business meetings and negotiations.

Methodology of the Study

To meet the objectives of the study both primary and secondary data were collected.

Primary data was collected by randomly meeting, listening and observing a couple of business professionals and observing various types of informal meetings and negotiations. All this was carried out during the five-day business trip to China between 28 Oct.–02 Nov., 2011. During the business conference, one got an opportunity to interact with a few Chinese professors. Lots of information was also collected during formal and informal interactions with many Chinese men and women (doing different types of businesses), while staying in the hotels of Shanghai and Beijing and also while shopping and sightseeing.

Secondary information was culled from various sources like documents, newspapers, books and existing literature.

- *Data Collection:* Information and data were collected from about 30 odd respondents based on availability. Out of these, four were business school professors, two were tourist guides, four were hotel officials, four were airport officials, two were taxi drivers and fourteen shopkeepers.

- *Data Analysis:* Qualitative analysis was carried out and quantitative analysis could not be done because of the small sample size.

Discussion of the Findings

Styles of Communication

Different aspects and styles of Chinese communication has been discussed under the following sub-headings like, *language, non-verbal communication and conduct.*

Language

In China, Mandarin is spoken across the nation. In all, over 1.2 billion people speak one or more varieties of Chinese. All varieties of the Chinese language belong to the Sino-Tibetan family of languages, and each one has its own dialects and sub-dialects, which are more or less mutually intelligible.

The number of Chinese who can speak English are however, increasing exponentially. Many Chinese have two names: One is of Chinese origin and the other is the adopted western name such as "Catherine" or "John." In smaller towns, the signages are usually written in Chinese.

Non-Verbal Communication

The Chinese non-verbal communication speaks volumes. Since the Chinese strive for harmony and are group dependent because of high contextualization, they also rely on facial expressions, tone of voice and posture to tell them what someone feels. Generally, Chinese try to maintain an impassive expression when someone is speaking. Frowning while someone is speaking is interpreted as a sign of disagreement. Chinese avoid eye contact in crowded situations to give themselves privacy. It is considered disrespectful to stare into another person's eyes.

Conduct

The Chinese give respect to age and seniority. This can be very well observed in their style of greetings, and communication- *Ni Hao* with a smile! People in China emphasize on "*Guanxi*" which means relationship. A display of negative emotions in public is considered inappropriate, and the Chinese are adept at masking their negative emotions. One should be careful when interpreting smiles. The Chinese love a good bargain: in the local markets, one can expect vigorous and exaggerated gestures during bargaining, which one need not take at face value.

Mannerisms at the Workplace

Mannerisms at the workplace vary from one context to another context, as they belong to different cultural groups. Because of high contextualization, the Chinese have a fixed set of mannerisms at the workplace, which are analyzed in the following paragraphs under sub-headings like, *Business dealings with new companies, Dining manners, Business dress code and Business cards.*

Business Dealings with New Companies

The Chinese do not do business with companies they do not know, because they cannot trust them. So, working through an intermediary is very important. This intermediary could be an individual or an organization, who can formally introduce and vouch for the reliability of the company.

Materials describing the company's history and literature about products and services in the Chinese language have to be sent well in advance. The Chinese often use intermediaries to ask questions that they would prefer not to ask directly.

Business relationships are built formally after the Chinese get to know you. Hence, patience is the key for conducting business. It takes a considerable amount of time, and is bound up with enormous bureaucracy.

The Chinese see foreigners as representatives of their company rather than as individuals. In business organizations the rank of professionals is extremely important in business relationships and one must keep rank differences in mind when communicating.

In business dealings there are no gender biases. It is also very important that one should never lose sight of the fact that communication is official, especially in dealing with someone of higher rank and seniority. Treating them too informally, especially in front of their peers, may eventually ruin a potential deal. The Chinese prefer face-to-face meetings rather than written or telephonic communication.

Meals and social events are not the place for business discussions. There is a demarcation between business and socializing in China, so care should be taken not to engage them together.

Dining Manners

There will be many servings of different dishes, and it is bad manners to refuse when something is being offered. It is best to eat small quantity so that one doesn't have to refuse food that comes later. As a foreigner, one is well regarded if one can eat with chopsticks.

Business Dress Code

The Chinese, like Indians, also dress conservatively, and both men and women wear formal western business suits at work. Business attire is conservative and unpretentious:

- Men should wear dark colored, conservative business suits.
- Women should wear conservative business suits or dresses with a high neckline.
- Women should wear flat shoes or shoes with very low heels.
- Bright colors should be avoided in formal meetings.

Business Cards

Business cards are exchanged after the initial introduction. Have one side of the business card translated into Chinese using simplified Chinese characters that are printed in gold ink since gold is an auspicious color. A business card should include one's title. If one's company is the oldest or largest in their respective country, that fact should be on your card as well. Hold the card in both hands when offering it, with the Chinese side facing the recipient. It is imperative to examine a business card before putting it on the table next to you, or in a business card case. Never write on someone's card unless so directed.

Business Meetings

Chinese business meetings do have a process and aim to cover all the points in the agenda. The following paragraphs describe Chinese business meetings in brief.

An appointment before every business meeting is necessary and, if possible, should be made between one-to-two months in advance, preferably in writing. If one does not have a contact within the company, an intermediary needs to be arranged for a formal introduction. Once the introduction has been made, one should provide the company with information and what needs to be accomplished in the meeting.

One should arrive at meetings on time, or slightly early. The Chinese view punctuality as a virtue. Arriving late is an insult and could negatively affect the business relationship. There is a need to pay great attention to the agenda, as each Chinese participant has his or her own agenda that they will attempt to introduce.

Circulating the agenda before the meeting gives Chinese colleagues a chance to meet with any technical experts prior to the meeting. It is a must to discuss and finalize the agenda with one's translator/ intermediary, prior to submission.

Each participant will take the opportunity to dominate the floor for lengthy periods without appearing to say very much of anything that actually contributes to the meeting. So, one has no other option but to be patient and listen. There could be subtle messages being transmitted that would assist you in allaying fears of an on-going association.

Business meetings require patience. Mobile phones ring frequently and conversations tend to be boisterous. Still it is advised never to ask the Chinese to turn off their mobile phones as this causes you both to lose face. Guests are generally escorted to their seats, which are in descending order of rank. Senior people generally sit opposite senior people from the other side.

It is imperative that you bring your own interpreter, especially if one plans to discuss legal or extremely technical concepts, as one can brief the interpreter prior to the meeting. Written material should be available in both English and Chinese, using simplified characters. One needs to be careful about what is written. It is essential that written translations are accurate which cannot be misinterpreted.

Visual aids are useful in large meetings and should only be done with black type on a white background. Colours have special meanings and if one is not careful, the colour choice could work against them. Presentations should be detailed and factual and focus on long-term benefits. Be prepared for the presentation to be a challenge.

Business Negotiations

In China, business negotiations are conducted very seriously and there are few norms which a negotiator should adhere to while in business. The next few paragraphs highlight Chinese negotiating styles.

During business negotiations only senior members of the negotiating team are supposed to speak. So, the most senior person in the group has to be designated as the spokesman for the introductory functions. Business negotiations occur at a slow pace. Be prepared for the agenda to become a jumping off point for other discussions. Chinese are non-confrontational. They will not overtly say 'no', they will say 'they will think about it' or 'they will see'.

Chinese negotiations are process oriented. They want to determine if relationships can develop to a stage where both parties are comfortable doing business with each other. Decisions may take a long time, as they require careful review and consideration.

Under no circumstances should one lose his or her temper, or one is bound to lose face and irrevocably damage the business relationship. One should not use high-pressure tactics. They might find themselves out maneuvered. Business is hierarchical. Decisions are unlikely to be made during the meetings you attend. The Chinese are shrewd negotiators. It could be worthwhile for the starting price to leave room for negotiations.

Implications of Findings

These findings will help one to understand why the Chinese styles of oral, nonverbal communication confirm to high contextualization, and how it is different from the low context group behavior. Conducting business is a process and takes a long time to conclude a deal. It is advisable for one to be patient and persuasive without losing temper and communicate assertively. Chinese negotiation tactics matches with the negotiation tactics carried out by the low context group which is matching the international standards of negotiation tactics.

According to a popular saying in China, it takes at least three generations to make a gentleman, so the challenge for the Chinese adopting global practices of business, or for others to do business in China—"the Chinese way" happens to be just a matter of time.

Suggestions of the Study

Based on the findings, the following suggestions have been presented that need to be contemplated by both the Chinese and the others for conducting global business.

- While English language is being taught and practiced at a faster pace in China, one needs to factor in the possibility of low penetration of the language while conducting business, as this could play a key role in obtaining better business results. Knowing a little Mandarin could help!
- One needs to be careful to not appear confrontational by staring down, or even looking directly at the Chinese for a long time. Non-verbal communication has to be more explicit in terms of eye contact.
- During business meetings, individuals should come prepared and try not to stray off from the agenda. It's best to have an all inclusive agenda if time is not a constraint, or else prioritization is the key.

Key Learnings from the Chinese Way of Doing Business

- To be sincere, hard working and loyal towards work.
- To not snub or belittle people in business meetings.
- To learn to be polite and patient.
- To learn not to lose temper while negotiating.

- To listen carefully and conduct business in a calm and composed manner.

Acknowledgements

Infrastructural support provided by the FORE School of Management, New Delhi in completing this article is gratefully acknowledged.

References

Engardio Pete; Chindia; Mc Graw-Hill, India, 2006.

Lehman, M. Carol; Dufrene, D. Debbie; Sinha Mala; Business Communication; Cengage Learning Pvt. Ltd., New Delhi, 2011.

China Daily, Nov. 01, 2011.

China Daily, Nov. 25–Dec. 01, 2011.

The Psychology of the Chinese Investor and Investment Decisions

Shalini Kalra Sahi

FORE School of Management, New Delhi

E-mail: skalrasahi@fsm.ac.in

ABSTRACT

The economic growth and expansion of financial markets, has given the Chinese consumer a number of investment products to choose from. Very few studies have been conducted on the Chinese financial consumer and on their investment decision making process. More such studies would enable a better understanding of the psychology of the Chinese investor, which will enable proper planning for the future needs of the investor, and facilitate in giving more personalized financial advice. This article presents some of the empirical work on the Chinese investor, and highlights the role of culture in the investment decision making process.

Keywords: China, Financial Consumer, Behavioral Biases, Behavioural Finance, Culture.

Introduction

The Chinese economy has undergone a major transition in recent years. With a GDP growth rate that was 9.1 percent[1] in 2011, and the average GDP growth rate between 2003 and 2010 being around 12.8 percent,[2] China's economy has emerged as one of the fastest growing economies in the world today. Further, gross saving

---

[1] http://data.worldbank.org/indicator/NY.GDP.MKTP.KD.ZG
[2] Datamonitor Country Insight Report China, 2011.

as a percentage of GDP for the year 2010, for China, was around 53 percent, as compared to India's 34 percent for the same time period.[3]

The average savings rate for urban households in China, with respect to their disposable income rose from 18 percent in 1995 to about 29 percent in 2009[4] and around 38 percent in 2010.[5] With such high savings rates, there would be a huge corpus of funds that find their way into various investment avenues. However, a question that arises here is that, are the savings finding their way into investments? This is of importance, as one of the major concerns for the Chinese economy is that "beginning in 2015, China will see a growing number of older citizens relying on a shrinking pool of young workers".[6] Hence, the working population today would need to save and invest for their future. Also, "For millennia, Confucian ethics in China placed *filial piety*—respect for one's elders—as a matter of cultural duty and obligation, including the duty to care for one's family in old age."[7] Hence, taking care of old age parents would involve planning for their medical expenses and insurance. By 2050, around 200 million people in China will be more than 60 years old.[8] Further, the one child policy that China put into place years ago has made people have smaller families, with a married couple having to take care of two sets of parents. Due to the poor social security system in the country, better investment planning and saving practices by the working population is needed, to enable a smooth flow of funds for fulfillment of the financial needs.

---

[3] http://data.worldbank.org/indicator/NY.GNS.ICTR.ZS

[4] http://www.voxeu.org/article/puzzle-china-s-rising-household-saving-rate

[5] http://www.washingtonpost.com/world/asia_pacific/getting-chinese-to-stop-saving-and-start-spending-is-a-hard-sell/2012/07/04/gJQAc7P6OW_story.html

[6] http://www.energybulletin.net/stories/2011-05-31/china-bubble-demographics-oldyoung-richpoor-urbanrural

[7] http://www.gsu.edu/38126.html

[8] http://www.china.org.cn/opinion/2012-06-13/content_25640362.htm

The financial services sector in China is quite young, and it is expanding at an increasing rate to meet the demands of the growing population. Eighty five percent of the finance for Chinese companies is provided by the banking sector in the country, which dominates the financial services sector.[9] With aplethora of financial products that are entering the Chinese financial marketplace, the consumer has to make decisions regarding investments, based on limited information and decision making abilities.

According to a KPMG report on China's capital markets—*The Changing Landscape (2011)*, the "total household savings in China hit RMB 31 trillion at the end of 2010, much of which has shifted between savings and stocks plus mutual funds" (p. 7). With these levels of savings, the requirements for wealth management services is expected to increase even further.[10] Herein, the role of understanding investor psychology becomes very pertinent. What can we understand about the psychology of the Chinese investor? What are the behavioural biases that Chinese investors exhibit when they make investment decisions?

This article is organized as follows: Section two, which consists of two sub-sections, dwells on the literature of the Chinese investors behaviour, and looks at the empirical work on the psychology of Chinese investors. Section three gives directions for further research and concludes the article.

Literature Review

Behavioural finance as a branch of finance, attempts to understand behaviours that people exhibit when making investment decisions. The studies under behavioural finance have a macro and a micro focus. While the macro aspect of behavioural finance looks at the

---

[9]www.ukti.gov.uk/.../FPS%20China%20opportunities%20sector%20b...
[10]http://blogs.ft.com/beyond-brics/2011/09/05/wealth-management-services-
  seduce-chinese-savers/#axzz1g8CkqbOc

psychology of financial markets, the micro aspect of behavioral finance looks at the individual investor.

The individual investor the world over, is exposed to a gamut of investment products to choose from, and is by the design of the human mind, prone to behavioural biases. These biases help the individuals to make sense of the information available, and speed up the decision making process. Apart from the various factors that influence investment choices of the individual, the culture to which the individual belongs also has a significant impact. The culture that a person belongs to defines the subconscious preferences that the individual has.

Statman (2008) conducted a study on countries and culture in behavioural finance and asked a very pertinent question "Do propensities for risk, regret, and maximization vary by country of origin?" (p. 38). He found that "people are affected by their cultures and experiences" (p. 8). Though studies in behavioural finance are plenty on American and European investors, very few studies are available on the Chinese financial consumer. The following sections present some of the studies on the psychology of the Chinese investor, and what these studies found.

Chinese Investor Behaviour and the Stock Market

The stock market shows the way for the manifestation of various behavioural biases in individuals. Various studies that have been conducted on Chinese investor behaviour in the stock market, show that investors exhibit various behavioural biases. An outline of some of these studies is presented in this section.

Chen, Kim, Nofsinger and Rui (2005) conducted a study on the brokerage account data from China, to understand the investing behavior and trading performance of Chinese investors. They found that Chinese investors exhibit an overconfidence bias, they are inclined towards the disposition effect and also have representativeness tendencies. Chen and Zhu (2005) in their study found that "investors in the Chinese stock market tend to under react to good news and over react to bad news" (p. 17).

Lucarelli and Palomba (2007) found that Chinese shareholders and their behavior in the stock markets are mostly driven by emotional behaviour. They found that the stock market returns are not influenced by the growth of the Chinese economy, but by the sentiments and the speculative tendencies of the investors.

Xindan and Bing (2008) studied the relationships between stock returns, their volatilities, and the individual investor sentiment in the Chinese stock market. They found that there was a positive relationship between changes in investor sentiments and stock returns, and that changes in sentiment were negatively correlated with market volatility.

Chinese Individual Investor Behaviour and Investment Decisions

Culture plays a paramount role in a Chinese individual's saving decisions, and the emphasis on planning for the long term is a trait that not only the Chinese inculcate in their youth, but so do other Asian countries (Harbaugh, 2004). In a study conducted by Statman (2008), respondents from 22 countries around the world were studied, to find out the influence of culture on various aspects of the investment decision making process. The propensities of the various cultures over six parameters were analyzed. The summary of the findings of the study with respect to China are presented in Table 1.

According to Statman's (2008) research, "China ranked the highest in agreeing that most people can be *trusted*" (p. 41). This can be explained by taking insights from the social structure that is prevalent in China called the *Guanxi* network.[11] The individual's

---

[11] http://chinese-school.netfirms.com/guanxi.html

Table 1: Ranking of the Propensities on Various
Parameters for the Chinese Sample

Variable	Chinese Sample (Ranking)
Propensity for taking risk in income	Highest rank
Propensity for taking risk in portfolio	Highest rank
Propensity for regret	Among the lowest ranks
Propensity for maximization	The lowest rank
Levels of happiness	Average
Trust	Highest rank

Source: Based on Statman (2008).

social network in China consists not just of "family, but also friends
and associates who might provide links to other associates who do
favours for one another" (Statman, 2008; p. 41). Since, the
Chinese deal with people based on their *Guanxi* network, *they lay
very high trust on the people who form part of their Guanxi.* Chan and
Chan (2011) studied the attitudes of Taiwanese nationals based in
China towards wealth management services and they found that,
*"Feeling of trustworthiness", "provision of flexible services," and
"Feeling of cultural affinity"* are the most crucial among ten factors
related to their intentions and decision making about choice of
wealth management service providers"(p. 272). Further, according
to Dang (2008) Chinese investors, "were more likely to hold stocks
if they had more knowledge, high risk tolerance, higher percentage
of assets invested in risky assets and *higher trust of security firms"* (p.
21). In these studies too, trust again comes out to be a significant
variable for the individual investors in China.

Statman (2008) also found that "China and Vietnam were the
most willing to take risks, and less prone to regret. Further, the
Chinese have the lowest propensity to achieve maximization. Fan
and Xiao (2003) had also studied cross cultural differences in risk,
and their results showed that the Chinese are more risk tolerant

than Americans in their financial decisions, both in attitudes and behavior. Hsee and Weber (1999) stated that, "people in a collectivist society, such as China, are more likely to receive financial help if they are in need, and consequently, they are less risk averse than those in an individualistic society such as the USA" (p. 165). Their study also found that the Chinese have more risk seeking tendencies as compared to the Americans. However, Chen, Kim, Nofsinger and Rui (2005) stated that while the Chinese people in general are more overconfident, however they view stock markets as risky, on account of the uncertainty that the stock market entails. This can also be explained by the fact that stock markets trading is of recent origin for Chinese investors, from around 1990, and hence many Chinese investors are still learning the nuances of stock markets. Further, Chinese society is a collectivist society and has low levels of individualism, as compared to countries like the USA and the UK. Hence, societies with high levels of individualism have a lower propensity for taking risk than a collectivist society like China (Hsee and Weber, 1999; Statman, 2008). This could also be explained with the *Guanxi* network theory, as the trust among the members is reasonably high, so that more risks can be taken, as support is ensured.

Wang, Qui and King (2010) conducted a study to find out the impact of a firm's CSR activities on Chinese investor behaviour. They found that "neither individual investors' nor institutional investors' behaviors are influenced by firms' CSR performance before the incident" (p. 127) However, when an event that draws the investor's attention to CSR activities occurs, "institutional investors' behaviors towards the company are significantly influenced by the firm's CSR performance that exceeds a certain threshold" (p. 127) Hence, Chinese investors do give emphasis to the CSR activities of a firm, for a short period of time, after an event occurs that brings into the limelight the importance of CSR. Thus, investing in companies that are more socially responsible is still low in China, as is also the case for many other countries.

The earlier literature shows that Chinese investors also exhibit biases that the literature on behavioural finance explains. Further, Chinese investors have a greater risk taking tendency as compared to their Western counterparts. Hence, the Chinese people have been found to have the highest propensity for risks despite having low per capita income levels, as per Statman (2008). This is quite interesting, as the general risk taking literature would differ on this view, as people with low per capita incomes would be expected to be risk averse. Further, Chinese investors put emphasis on trust as a very important factor when it comes to investment decisions. Both these aspects find explanations in the fact that Chinese deal with people on their '*Guanxi* Network' and that it is still a collectivist Chinese society. These insights draw attention to the role of Chinese culture in investment decision making of Chinese investors. Further, though the findings of the studies do show that Chinese investors behaviour differs in some aspects as compared to investors from other countries, on account of culture, yet, the number of studies on Chinese investors are very limited for developing a comprehensive picture of the Chinese financial consumer.

Future Directions for Research and Conclusion

Given the insights from the literature review, it can be seen that culture plays a very important role in individual investor behaviour. Very few studies have been conducted on the Chinese financial consumer, and further studies would enable financial service providers in China to better understand Chinese investors and give advice that suits the needs of investors. By incorporating the insights from such studies, better financial advisory services can be given to enable Chinese financial consumers to be satisfied financially. Further, companies that enter Chinese markets, would gain from the insights of such studies, which would help them to better understand Chinese investor behaviour.

References

Chan, C. and Chan, A. (2011). "Attitude toward wealth management services: Implications for international banks in China", *International Journal of Bank Marketing*, Vol. 29, Issue 4, pp. 272–292.

Chen, G.-M., Kim, K.A., Nofsinger, J.R. and Rui, O.M. (2005). Behavior and performance of emerging market investors: Evidence from China, October 2005, available online: http://ccfr.org.cn/cicf2006/cicf2006paper/20060104133427.pdf.

Chen, M.W. and Zhu, J. (2005). Do Investors in Chinese Stock Market Overreact? *Journal of Accounting and Finance Research*, Vol. 13, No. 3, pp. 17–25.

Dang, W. (2008). Factors Affecting consumers' stock ownership decisions in China. ProQuest Dissertations and Theses; Master's Dissertation submitted to Department of Agribusiness and Agricultural Economics, University of Manitoba, Winnipeg.

Fan, J.X. and Xiao, J.J. (2005). A Cross-Cultural Study in Risk Tolerance: Comparing Chinese and Americans .Available at SSRN: http://ssrn.com/abstract=939438

Harbaugh, R. (2004). "China's high savings rates", Paper prepared for conference on "The rise of China revisited: Perception and reality", National Chengchi University, Taiwan.

Hsee, Christopher K. and Elke U. Weber. (1999). "Cross-National Differences in Risk Preferences and Lay Predictions." *Journal of Behavioral Decision Making*, Vol. 12, No. 2 (May): 165–179.

KPMG report on China's Capital Markets—The changing landscape (2011), Available at http://www.kpmg.com/CN/en/IssuesAndInsights/Articles Publications/Documents/China-Capital-Markets-FTSE-201106. pdf

Lucarelli, C. and Palomba, G. (2007). Investors' Behaviour in the Chinese Stock; Exchanges: Empirical Evidence in a Systemic; Approach, No. 297, Working Papers, Universita' Politecnica delle Marche (I), Dipartimento di Scienze Economiche e Sociali.

Statman, M. (2008). "Countries and Culture in Behavioral Finance", *CFA Institute Conference Proceedings Quarterly*, September, pp. 38–44.

Wang, M., Qiu, C. and Kong, D. (2010). Corporate Social Responsibility, Investor Behaviors, and Stock Market Returns: Evidence from a Natural Experiment in China. *Journal of Business Ethics,* (2011) 101: 127–141.

Xindan, L. and Bing, Z. (2008). Stock market behavior and investor sentiment: Evidence from China Frontiers of Business Research in China, Vol. 2, No. 2, pp. 277–282.

"Operations" Acumen from Sun Tzu's "Art of War"

Mohita G. Sharma

FORE School of Management, New Delhi
E-mail: mohita@fsm.ac.in

ABSTRACT

Sun Tzu's "Art of War" is almost 2,500 years old Chinese military treatise, and is used widely in military education. Its implications in business strategy are also well established. This article tries to appreciate the acumen that can be derived from these powerful quotes to guide the operations strategy aspects of business.

Keywords: Art of War, Operations, Strategy.

Introduction

Sun Tzu was a philosopher, thinker, mentor who lived in the present Shangdong Province around 500 B.C. "Tzu" was a title conferred on him which meant a "master." He belongs to the same period as Confucius, and they were the first consultants in history. Chinese society is didactic and derives maxims from these philosopher-consultants-mentors. Incidentally, this is one of the rare books of the times which is available. It finds wide applications in the military environment and has been widely accepted in business strategy. This article tries to interpret this acumen for business operations.

Literature Review

Although there has been ample literature motivated by SunTsu's *Art of War in Business Strategy* like Wu et.al (2005) and in other functional areas. The organizational and people aspect has been studied by Fernandez (2004). Foo (2004) derives inspiration for the systems perspective of business. Shung et.al (2012) looks at the analytics perspective. Hence, it addresses the "operations" aspects of business which has not been analysed in the literature.

Interpretations

In this section of the article, the principles in the book have been quoted alongwith the interpretation and deduction for business operations strategy. The book is concise and precise and provides only ideas. Interpretation is the creativity of the individual (Khoo, 1992). This article goes through the book with an '"operations management' lens.

1. The Concept of Triple—A operations (Agile, Adaptable and Aligned) has analogies available in the Sun Tsu's work.

*Agile: (*The system quickly responds to sudden changes in supply and demand. It handles unexpected external disruptions smoothly and cost-efficiently. And it recovers promptly from shocks such as natural disasters, epidemics and computer viruses).

"Those who are skilled in military operations should be as dextrous as the shuairan, the snake of Mount Chang. If you strike its head, its tail will launch an attack on you; if you hit its tail, its head will strike you; if you beat its body, it will attack with both its head and tail."

This is the essence of agility. Snake can be a metaphor for agility. In all unpredictable situations, system operations should not crash. As the volatility of the market and demand increases and unpredictability of events increase, the need of operations to be resilient enough cannot be debated. This could be implemented through proper flow of information between suppliers and customers, collaborative relationship with suppliers, building inventory buffers by maintaining a stockpile of inexpensive but key components, dependable logistics system or partner, contingency plans to develop crisis management teams etc.

Adaptable: (Adjust operations according to market demand).

"As water shapes its flow in accordance with the ground, so an army manages its victory in accordance with the situation of the enemy."

Water exemplies adaptability. As economic progress, political shifts, demographic trends, and technological advances reshape markets, monitor economies all over the world to spot new supply bases and markets. Use intermediaries to develop fresh suppliers and logistics. Create flexible product designs. Determine where companies' products stand in terms of technology cycles and product life cycles.

Alignment: (They align the interests of all participating firms with their own).

"We cannot enter into alliance with neighbouring princes until we are acquainted with their designs. We are not fit to lead an army on the march unless we are familiar with the face of the country—its mountains and forests, its pitfalls and precipices, its marshes and swamps. We shall be unable to turn natural advantages to account unless we make use of local guides."

Exchange of information and knowledge freely with vendors and customers forms the guiding principles for alignment. Equitably share risks, costs and gains of improvement initiatives. The concept of "We are in this together" has to be nurtured.

2. Concept of Theory of Constraints':

"On the field of battle, the spoken word does not carry far enough: hence the institution of gongs and drums. Nor can ordinary objects be

seen clearly enough: hence the institution of banners and flags. Gongs and drums, banners and flags, are means whereby the ears and eyes of the host may be focused on one particular point. In night-fighting, then, make much use of signal-fires and drums, and in fighting by day, of flags and banners, as a means of influencing the ears and eyes of your army."

In operations terminology, we can draw a parallel to the approach of synchronisation. This can be further elaborated as the Drum-Buffer-Rope Approach or the Theory of Constraints. 'Bottleneck' is the one single point where the focus of the system has to be maintained. The drum has to beat to the rhythm of the bottleneck, and all the other elements have to follow. The rope as a result of the drum is pulled, and the production system is geared to provide resources for the bottleneck. The buffer is essential in order, to ensure that the bottleneck is always busy and in full supply. The *drum* is the physical constraint of the plant: the work centre, or machine, or operation that limits the ability of the entire system to produce more. The rest of the plant follows the beat of the drum. They make sure the drum has work, and that anything the drum has processed, does not get wasted. The *buffer* protects the drum, so that it always has work flowing to it. The *rope* is the work release mechanism for the plant. The Drum-Buffer-Rope method strives to achieve the y reliable due-date performance, effective exploitation of the constraint, and as short a response time as possible, within the limitations imposed by the constraint.

3. Concept of Rapid-Fire Fulfilment:

"Let your rapidity be that of the wind, your compactness that of the forest. At first assume the coyness of a maiden and when the enemy gives you an opening, attack him as swiftly as a running hare."

This tenet can be understood in terms of the strategy of rapid fire fulfilment. This wants the system to be super responsive, rather than efficient. This means being ready to be more responsive at times, at the expense of cost. This concept talks of leveraging the assets to provide flexibility. The compactness refers to 'density' or 'firmness' which swiftly transforms into uninterrupted supply.

4. Concept of Lean:

"An army cannot survive without its equipment, food and stores. The skilful general does not require a second levy of conscripts, or more than one provisioning."

This principle leads to the concept of "Lean". The dedication of fewer inputs and stress on reducing waste, is the spirit of going "lean."

5. Concept of Chaos:

"Amid the turmoil and tumult of battle, there may be seeming disorder and yet no real disorder at all; amid confusion and chaos, your array may be without head or tail, yet it will be proof against defeat. Simulated disorder postulates perfect discipline, simulated fear postulates courage; simulated weakness postulates strength."

This dictum indicates to the use of the Chaos theory, which can be utilized in operations strategy. Chaos theory provides a useful theoretical framework. All organisations can be modelled as complex, dynamic systems which exhibit uncertainty. But, if this uncertainty can be simulated, an underlying order can be identified. E.g. the supply chain reflects a total chaotic system. But, by conceptualizing a chaotic system, managerial implications can be defined. By understanding the degree of freedom and discerning the underlying pattern, short term guidelines can be laid down.

Observing pattern is useful, because then different phases of the system and characteristics can be associated. An unique aspect of these patterns is that they are scale independent. A further derivative of this idea could be: 'To be able to create chaos with an underlying order and use it as a strategy.'

6. Concept of Self Assessment:

"The skilful warriors in ancient times first made themselves invincible and then awaited the enemy's moment of vulnerability. Invincibility depends on oneself, but the enemy's vulnerability on himself."

This dictum drives us to appreciate that the first exercise of an operations analyst is "Self assessments". The strength of any operations is equal to the strength of the "weakest links."

Only after finding and fixing your weakest link, can one look outward.

7. Concept of Analytics:

The elements of the art of war are first, the measurement of space; second, the estimation of quantities; third, the calculation of figures; fourth, comparisons of strength and fifth, chances of victory.

In respect of military method, we have, first, Measurement; second, Estimation of quantity; third, Calculation; fourth, Balancing of chances; fifth, Victory.

Measurement owes its existence to Earth; Estimation of quantity to measurement; Calculation to estimation of quantity; Balancing of chances to calculation; and victory to Balancing of chances.

This tenet indicates the stress on 'analytics'. It is not possible to compete on products or services alone. Being an 'analytics competitor' provides a competitive edge. Using sophisticated techniques to collect data and interpreting and exploiting all possible inferences that can provide value to the business. To do so, an analytics culture has to be developed which shall respect measuring, testing and evaluating quantitative evidence. Decision making should be supported by numbers. The initiative should be spearheaded from the top and it should be under one leadership.

Conclusion

The study and analysis of the dictums indicate that there is an analogy which can be derived with business operations which can sharpen our business acumen. Although the dictums are not applicable verbatim, but the idea of this article is to derive the spark for igniting operations strategic thinking. Future research can include many other great ancient Chinese scholars like Confucius, Tao whose work can provide inspiration for business.

Acknowledgement

I acknowledge my Institute, FORE School of Management for providing me the opportunity to have firsthand experience of China, and interacting with the Chinese academicians which provided me with a holistic appreciation of their environment, culture, business and education perspective.

References

Fernandez, J.A., "Management in times of change: Lesssons from The Art of War" Business Strategy Review, Spring 2004, Vol. 15, No. 1, pp. 51–58.

Foo, C.T., "The Art of War: The System of Systems Engineering Perspective", Chinese Management Studies, Spring 2004, Vol. 2, No. 4, pp. 317–326.

Shung, P.K. and Junyu, C.M., "Applications of Analytics in Business Strategy", *Business Intelligence Journal*, Jan. 2012, Vol. 5, No. 1, pp. 190–194.

Khoo, K.H. (1992). Sun Tzu and Management, Pelanduk Publications (M) Sdn bhd. Kualalumpur.

Wu, W.Y., Chou, C.H., Wu, Y.J., "A study of strategy implementation as expressed through Sun Tsu's principles of war. " Industrial Management and Data Systems, 2004, Vol. 104(5), pp. 396–408.

From Bounded Feet to Fleet-footed: The Chinese Women's Journey towards Equality

Sanghamitra Buddhapriya

FORE School of Management, New Delhi

E-mail: sanghamitra@fsm.ac.in

ABSTRACT

Chinese women have made their mark on the global stage. In a relatively short time, they have left their dependent and subservient image behind and come up as equal partners in a male-dominated society. The post-revolutionary Chinese state has enabled Chinese women through successive constitutional and legal measures, to play their due role in all spheres of their lives. The economic reforms since the 1980s have created the necessary conditions for women's rise as a productive force. They are establishing themselves as self-made entrepreneurs and as successful business leaders. However, they are grossly underrepresented in the higher echelons, as well as in the political field. The traditional Oriental and Confucian values with their emphasis on masculine superiority have continued to inhibit their rise in certain areas. In addition to state sponsored initiatives, efforts need to be made at the societal level, to take this wonderful journey of Chinese women forward in the right direction.

Keywords: *Stereotypes, Confucian Values, Self-made Female Entrepreneurs, Women Liberation.*

Introduction

Chinese society had traditionally been patriarchal, where women were treated as subservient to men until a few decades ago. The practice of foot-binding, where the arch of a woman's foot was broken and the toes were wrapped up against the foot, to create a smaller looking foot with an acute arch, primarily to make the feet look attractive and arousing for men, epitomised the social outlook regarding women in China, until the early twentieth century. With the coming of the Communist revolution, the conservative ethos of the Confucian era was actively discouraged, thanks to a complete overhaul of the socio-economic structure which deemphasised "old ideas, habits, customs and cultures" (the four olds). Women in China have since managed to establish their position in Chinese society. So much so that today, out of the top ten richest self-made women in the world, six are Chinese and interestingly, they occupy the first three positions as well.[1] The present article seeks to trace this astounding journey of Chinese women, from being looked upon as objects of desire, to establishing their role as successful business leaders and entrepreneurs. It also makes an attempt to critically analyse their position in Chinese society today.

The Revolution and After: Supportive Measures

Prior to the Communist revolution, the popular disillusionment with traditional Confucian culture had poured out into the streets in May 1919, following the failure of the Chinese Republic, founded in 1912 to address China's problems. There was a popular demand for creation of a new culture based on global and western values. The leaders of the 'new culture movement' demanded a thorough reexamination of Confucian ethics and among others, an end to the patriarchal family system, and the recognition of progressive values like individual freedom and women's liberation.

---

[1]Allison Jackson, "China dominates richest self-made women list", Oct 11, 2010 As per report by Associate Free Press, available at: http://www.google. com/hostednews/afp/article/ALeqM5i9IzJJRLqVcsm8fnxYx8hRTfxSKQ?docI d=CNG.08f7f85b62df316e015d94739f07df92.8c1

This movement prepared the grounds for the Communist revolution. Immediately after coming to power in 1949, the Communist government actively promoted social, economic and political roles of women in Chinese society. A common programme with the status of a provisional constitution was adopted, which stipulated that women enjoyed equal rights with men in all aspects of life. Soon afterwards, the All-China Women's Federation was established. The most revolutionary step taken by the government, was the promulgation and implementation of the Marriage Law in 1950. This law abrogated the regressive marriage systems prevalent in China until then, which held women as inferior to men, and put into practice the new system of monogyny and equality of the sexes.[2]

The first Constitution of the People's Republic of China promulgated in 1954, reinforced the measures taken earlier, and clearly stipulated that women should enjoy equal rights with men in all aspects of life, i.e., in political, economic, cultural, social and family life. In 1980, a New Marriage Law revised the 1950 Marriage Law, and made it even more favourable for women. In the same year, China signed the International Convention on the Elimination of All Forms of Discrimination against Women and the principles enumerated in this Convention were translated into Chinese and disseminated amongst the public for popular education and awareness. In the same year also, four Special Economic Zones were established, with emphasis on export production in areas such as textiles and shoes, toys and electronics, where preference was given to women for their 'nimble fingers.'[3] In 1982, the Constitution was revised to accommodate the principle of 'equal remuneration

---

[2]Data used in this article from Chinese government sources are taken from the publication titled "*Women and Men in China: Facts and Figures 2004*", Department of Population, Social Science and Technology, National Bureau of Statistics, Government of China. Available at: http://www.stats.gov.cn/english/statisticaldata/otherdata/men&women_en.pdf

[3]Christa Wichterich (2009), "*Trade—A Driving Force for Jobs and Women's Empowerment?* Focus on China and India, FES Briefing Papers, Berlin.

for women and men workers for work of equal value.' New provisions were added to protect the institutions of marriage and family, and to prohibit 'maltreatment of old people, women and children'.

In 1985, the state went further and adopted the Law of Inheritance, Article 9 of which stipulated that women and men were equal in their rights to inheritance. During the same year, Standard and Requirement of Health Care for Pregnant Women in Urban and Rural Areas was issued by the Ministry of Public Health. The General Rules of the Civil Law in 1986 legalised equal civil rights for women, and prohibited all forms of arbitrary marriages. The Law of Compulsory Education in the same year, stipulated that all children from the age of six would go to school, to obtain compulsory education for a certain number of years, regardless of sex, ethnic group or race.

The reforms of the 1980s culminated in an amendment to the Chinese Constitution in 1988 which legalized private business activities. Interestingly, in 1989, 90,581 private enterprises were registered in China. Thus, from the mid 1980s, private business activities were first tolerated "and later encouraged because they created jobs and supplied goods and services." Chinese entrepreneurs made good use of these opportunities and "by the end of 1986, the Chinese media was reporting that there were 12 million licensed entrepreneurs of whom 8 million were women.[4]

In 1988, Regulations on Labour Protection of Women Employees was issued by the State Council, and later that year, the Ministry of Labour issued a circular on Issues of Treatment of Childbearing Employees. In 1990, the same ministry issued an order regulating work restricted for women employees. In 1992, the government

---

[4]*Xinhua*, December 3, 1986, cited in Beverley M. Kitching, "*Female Entrepreneurs in Transitional Economies: a comparative study of Businesswomen in Nigeria and China*", 2004, available at http://eprints.qut.edu.au/1168/1/1168.pdf

passed the law Protecting the Legal Rights and Interests of Women which "specified, systemized and regularized the regulations concerning the rights and interests of women stipulated in the Constitution, and various laws through articles of guarantee, coordination, sanction and supplementation."

The Coordinating Committee on Women and Children was changed into the National Working Committee on Women and Children (NWCCW) in 1993. Based on its recommendations, the new revised Law of Labour was adopted in 1994 with specific regulations for protection of women, especially during menstruation, as well as childbearing and breast-feeding phases. Following the fourth "*World Conference on Women*" in Beijing in September 1995, the NWCCW pushed for NPA for women as a follow-up activity, to ensure achievement of the goals set by the conference and emphasised its implementation especially in the rural underdeveloped pockets. A working group for monitoring and evaluation of the NPA for women was setup under the NWCCW in 1997.

In 1998, the Program for the Development of Chinese Women and Children 2001–2010 was formulated at the 8th National Conference of *Women Representatives of China*. The programme sought to further implement the policy of equality of women and men, to further optimize the environment of living, protection and development for women and children, to further "authorize women with equal rights in political, economic, cultural, social and family affairs, to improve the general quality of women's life, to achieve overall progress of women by wide participation." After thorough discussions and debate at the national level, the 37th Standing Committee of the State Council reviewed and approved this programme, and it was implemented in May 2001. China became a WTO member in November 2001, and subsequently, new forward-looking global trade rules were established in China regarding foreign and domestic investments. In 2005, the government amended the landmark 1992 Law on the Protection of Women's Rights and Interests, which is known as the Women's Constitution, and made gender equality an explicit state policy. It also outlawed, for the first time, sexual harassment.

Things have looked up for women in China because of such regular governmental emphasis on taking measures to develop their condition on the one hand, and by creating enabling conditions for their rise as an economic force, on the other.

The State of the Women in China

China has taken steps to address the issue of women illiteracy. Before 1949, the overall illiteracy rate was above 80 percent and women's illiteracy rate was as high as 90 percent. By 2002, the overall illiteracy rate had dropped to 9.16 percent- 4.99 percent for men and 13.5 percent for women. The 1990s witnessed a dramatic rise in women's education at the post-secondary level. In 2003, the proportion of female students in regular higher education institutes was about 44.8 percent (Ministry of Education of China, 2004). This explains the rising influx of women into the workforce during the same period.

In 1949, when the government took the first step forward to improve the condition of women in Chinese society, women constituted seven percent of the total workforce. By 1992, the percentage rose to 38 percent. Women's contribution to family income went up from 20 percent in the 1950s to 40 percent in the 1990s. In 1982, Chinese working women constituted 43 percent of the total workforce, compared to 35 percent in the USA and 36 percent in Japan.[5] Women are playing an increasingly important role in China. Women's employment is concentrated in farming,

---

[5]C.C. Chen, and KC Yu, and JB Miner, (1997). "Motivation to Manage: A Study of Women in Chinese State-Owned Enterprises", *The Journal of Applied Behavioral Science*, Vol. 33, No. 2, p. 160.

forestry, animal husbandry and fisheries, manufacturing, wholesale and retail sales trade, and catering, education, culture, arts and broadcasting, films and TV.[6]

Change in Women's Worldview

As per surveys conducted by the government, Chinese women have been more mobile than ever before, and about 34.6 percent women have been to provinces other than their home provinces, or abroad. 53.6 percent of rural women have also been to big and medium-sized cities outside of their hometowns in search of employment. In urban pockets, Chinese women are claiming new status and power due to their growing earning power. Women are more satisfied with life than before. 93.2 percent of women are very satisfied or relatively satisfied with their marriage and family life; 77.3 percent are satisfied with marital life; and 67.6 percent are very satisfied or relatively satisfied with their cultural life, compared to 10 years ago. Women's capabilities have been widely recognized. 82 percent of women surveyed were "confident in themselves," and most of the interviewees (66 percent) disagreed with the saying that "men are born to be more capable than women."

Women today are more willing than ever to work and earn. Among all interviewees, 88 percent of the women expressed their strong desire to work, even though their spouses either earned more, or their family owned enormous wealth. Their self-awareness has increased. 57.2 percent of the women interviewed in 2000 disagreed with the viewpoint that "It is better for women to marry successfully than to work successfully." In line with these changes, the traditional worldview about woman's role is also undergoing a marked change. 82.3 percent of the interviewees for example, expressed agreement or strong agreement with the view that "men should undertake half the household chores."

---

[6] Ibid. note 2.

Two Distinct Phases

As per the study by Li Xiaojiang (2000), an eminent scholar on women's studies in China,[7] women's liberation took place in two distinct phases. The first phase, from 1949 to 1976, witnessed Chinese women being liberated as a whole group, "holding half of the sky" as Mao put it. They were treated as equal with men, and included even in the jobs that required the most stringent physical labour. The second phase, which began from 1977 and continues till date, has seen the rise of women as liberated individuals, and not as members of a socially backward group. During the latter phase, Chinese women were integrated with the wider world and participated in international women's movements. The first phase, Li says, was the most crucial, because it helped Chinese women to free themselves from socially imposed shackles and recognize their innate potentials. In the second phase, their sense of liberation went beyond seeking equality with men. Chinese women sought to discover their individuality beyond their gendered identity.

Most Number of Richest Self-Made Women

This explains the fact that half of the world's richest self-made women are Chinese. The Hurun Rich List[8] for the year 2011 listed 156 women among 1000 richest people from China. The average age of the 50 richest Chinese women is 48, three years younger than the overall figure of the Hurun Rich List 2011. Thirty-three of the 50 richest Chinese women are self-made (Yuan) billionaires,

---

[7]Li Xiaojiang (2000), "Fifty Years, How Far Have We Reached: Reflection on the Liberation and Development of Chinese Women", cited in Jing Lin, "Chinese Women Under the Economic Reform, Gains and Losses", *Harvard Asia Pacific Review*, p.90, available at: http://web.mit.edu/lipoff/www/hapr/summer03_security/LIN.pdf

[8]For details see http://www.hurun.net/usen/NewsShow.aspx?nid=151

up from 30 in the year 2010.[9] In 2010, China had the most self-made women entrepreneurs in the world, and 11 of the top 20 wealthiest self-made women in the world.[10] Another interesting statistic pertaining to Chinese women, is the rise in the sale of luxury cars like Maserati, Maranello, Ferrari, Lamborghini etc. Women account for about 20 percent of mainland sales of Ferrari and 30 percent of Maserati.[11]

The surge in China's wealthy women is often ascribed to their "intense work ethic and strong ambition." According to a study by the Center for Work-Life Policy, just over one-third of all college-educated American women describe themselves as very ambitious, versus two thirds in China.[12] This report says that 76 percent of women in China aspire to hold a top corporate job, compared to 52 percent in the US. One of the more interesting findings from the study was, that Communism may have given women a boost, because it underscored that women could do whatever men could do.

The report indicated that like their Western counterparts, Chinese women are now graduating at nearly the same rate as men (47 percent). In China today, women account for nearly 40 percent of the total MBA students enrolled in the top-ranked programmes at the China Europe International Business School in Shanghai and Tsinghua University (popularly hailed as the Chinese MIT). Sixty-five percent of the more than 1,000 college-educated women surveyed, consider themselves very ambitious, compared to 36 percent of their counterparts in the US.

---

[9] See the report "Hurun releases list of richest Chinese women", September 29, 2011, available at http://www.china.org.cn/china/2011-09/29/content_23515322.htm

[10] See report at: http://english.peopledaily.com.cn/90001/90776/90882/7164199.html

[11] See report at http://www.omaha.com/article/20110118/NEWS03/701189913

[12] For this report see: http://www.worklifepolicy.org/documents/CWLP - China Study press release final.pdf

Reasons for their Success

In a traditional oriental society like that of China, where women were treated as mere appendages of men, the measures initiated by the Communist government acted as a major catalyst for change. It broke open the traditional barriers, and brought into operation, in a comparatively more effective manner than in other oriental societies, a slew of legal and constitutional measures which made gender based discrimination increasingly difficult. Moreover, the economic reforms that came by since the 1980s, prepared the grounds for private initiatives in the Chinese economy, and by actively encouraging female entrepreneurship through supportive training, education and allocation of resources for investment. The new social environment, the changing demographic conditions and shifting emphases while making personal choices, have also played their role in launching the new generation of Chinese women on the path of liberation and economic progress.

As the statistics reveal, a majority of Chinese female entrepreneurs come from the age group of 5–44. There is an increasing emphasis on education and knowledge, work-family balance, and carving out a successful career path both as entrepreneurs and as employees. There is also a view that the women are where they are in China because of the "poverty push," rather than the "opportunity pull."[13] Others regard essential Chinese Confucian values like "tolerance of others, harmony with others and contentedness," helped Chinese women in transiting from their traditional home bound role, to the realm of competitive economy. Confucian emphasis on qualities like persistence, thrift, order among relationships, as well as having a sense of shame, saving face and respect for traditions also contributed the development of the business environment in

---

[13]Y. Zhang (2003). *Enterprise founded by entrepreneurs and its growth*, Tianjin, China: Nankai University Press.

China.[14] These values "certainly help Chinese women entrepreneurs to formulate harmonious corporate cultures, which may well be the basis of their high success rate as a result of satisfied employees and customers," according to some observers.[15]

Challenges

In spite of such remarkable progress in the socio-economic sphere made by Chinese women, potential challenges remain. In spite of years of reforms and active promotion of egalitarian and libertarian values, negative stereotypes about women persist to this day. In fact, some analyses suggest that with the gradual reduction of emphasis on socialism and socialist values, "powerful cultural traditions that value men over women, long held in abeyance by official Communist support for women's rights, [have] return[ed] in force."[16]

There is a marked preference for male children. The reported sex ratio at birth is quite high at about 119 males to 100 female births. The preference for sons has skewed the sex ratio at birth in favour of males. Moreover, most Chinese men expect their wives to take care of home and family, even if it may often lead to work-family conflict. With the growing number of aged population in China, family responsibility includes caring for elderly parents or relatives,

---

[14]P. Gerrard, H. Schoch and B. Cunningham (2003). "Values and skills of female entrepreneurs in Vietnam: an exploratory study", *Asia Pacific Business Review*, Vol. 10, No. 2, pp. 138–159.

[15]Ilan Alon, Shengliang Deng and Xu Wang, "Framework for female entrepreneurship in China", *International Journal of Business and Emerging Markets*, Vol. 3, No. 1, p. 19.

[16]Didi Kirsten Tatlow, "For China's Women, More Opportunities, More Pitfalls", *The New York Times*, November 25, 2010. Available at http://www.nytimes.com/2010/11/26/world/asia/26iht-china.html?adxnnl=1&partner=rss&emc=rss&adxnnlx=1323871369-8QJJaOGB/Sxmpa9zC7cJpw

in addition to raising children.[17] Hence their responsibilities do not stop when the children grow up. The social pressures on this count can be so forbidding that they discourage women to work.

Many employers are not hiring women workers, because that may force them to spend more in the form of maternity leave and childbirth costs, because Chinese laws now stipulate that employers will have to cover those costs. Many observers say that gender based discrimination is widespread in China. Despite the prevalence of a law favouring them, most women do not dare to sue their employers for unfair hiring practices, dismissal on grounds of pregnancy or maternity leave, or sexual harassment. Moreover, the laws also reinforce societal biases by prescribing that women would retire five years earlier than men at the same jobs, which significantly reduces their earnings and pensions. Government data also admits that the salaries of women is generally lower than men in all industries. The largest gap is found in the mining and public service industries, where the salary of women is about 74 percent that of men.

The representation of women in the political sphere has been visibly low. As per the data provided by the Chinese National Bureau of Statistics, among all members of the Political Bureau of the Communist Party of China (CPC) and national government only seven are women. Among Ministers and Vice-Ministers 14 are women; among the leading cadres at the ministerial level, 48 are women. Among the leading groups of government and Communist party committees at the provincial, prefectural and county levels, 56, 647 and 4,353 are women respectively. National Peoples' Congress has only about 604 women out of its total representatives of 2987. In Chinese People's Political Consultative Conference there are only 375 (16.8 percent) women representatives. There is a

---

[17]"Women in China, The sky's the limit but it's not exactly heaven", Special Report, *The Economist*, November 26, 2011. Available at http://www.economist. com/node/21539931

tame acknowledgement by the Chinese government that in general, "the political participation of women in China is still relatively low in all levels of government."

Chinese women prefer to work in state-owned companies, because these are relatively comfortable places to work especially at the lower levels, with shorter and more predictable hours than in the private sector. But, there also the attitudes remain highly conservative and very few women are found at the senior management level.[18] Frank's (2001) survey among Chinese students majoring in management finds that there was a stereotypical perception of women as more incompetent, slower, weaker, more followers-than-leaders, more lenient, more democratic, less active and more friendly than male managers. Therefore, many women workers in China today find it easier to work with multinational companies, because there is less sexual discrimination than in Chinese concerns.

Conclusion

Chinese women have come a long way since the Communist revolution. However, they still have lots of grounds to cover. While their presence in the workforce has increased manifold, traditional barriers stand in the way of their rising to the top. The governmental document on women published in 2004 recognised the fact that:

> ...cultural and conceptual sediments of thousands of years of feudal ideology cannot be weeded out in a short time. In reality, many issues of women's development are still hampering a healthy social development. For example, participation by women in management of state and social affairs is still at a low level; it is difficult for laid-off women to find re-employment; the rights of women for land contracts

---

[18]Ellen J. Frank (2001). "Chinese students' perceptions of women in management: will it be easier?", *Women In Management Review*, Vol. 16, No. 7, pp. 316–324.

are violated in some areas; domestic violence and some criminal activities against women's personal rights still occur."

The top-down approach through initiation of governmental measures to bring about a change in societal perception about women has succeeded in laying the foundations of a favourable work environment for women. Such state-driven initiatives will have to be complemented by efforts at the civil societal level, to alter stereotypical perceptions of women as subservient to men.

Infrastructure Growth in China: The Good, The Bad and The Ugly

Qazi Asif Zameer

FORE School of Management, New Delhi

E-mail: asif@fsm.ac.in

ABSTRACT

China is at the center of the global economy today. It has been the fastest growing economy for a considerable period now, and is the country with the largest foreign exchange reserves. Since China embarked on the path of globalization and liberalization around twenty seven years back, its infrastructure has grown at an amazing pace. The speed and scale of projects like highways, bridges, fast speed railway links, ports, airports, high-rises has left the entire world amazed, and in awe of Chinese efficiency. However, some experts and observers have started questioning the strength, quality and durability of these constructions. Other social scientists have produced research papers and articles about the immense social cost of these projects, in terms of forceful acquisition of land, displacement of innumerable villages, poor resettlement policies and quashing of all resistance by the Chinese government with an iron fist. This article paper tries to assimilate the data from various secondary sources about the great achievements of Chinese infrastructure builders over the last two decades, as well as show the dark side of this growth story.

Keywords: China, Infrastructure, Growth, Problems.

Background

The moment you step out of the international airport in Shanghai, you are likely to be overcome by a serious inferiority complex (especially if you are an Indian). You start wondering whether any of the Indian cities will be like this even in the next fifty years; probably not. The gleaming high-rises, the mosaic of overlapping flyovers, the glistening tarmac of the roads, the magnitude of traffic without any chaotic traffic jams, the superstores of Wal-Mart, Tesco, Carrefour etc.—all showcase China's financial might, and are designed to mesmerize the visitors.

But, is everything as good as it seems in the Dragon's Heaven? The study done by the author revealed many layers in this story of amazing growth of infrastructure in China, which the following passages are meant to highlight.

The Good

- In July 2011, political celebrations for the 90th anniversary of the Chinese Communist Party coincided with the unveiling of three mega-projects: 1) the world's longest sea bridge, which spans 16 miles (26 km) from Qingdao to Huangdao; 2) the world's longest gas pipeline, which stretches 5,400 miles (8,700 km) from Xingjiang to Guangzhou; and 3) a new high-speed railway, which cuts travelling time between Beijing and Shanghai to less than five hours. [Jonathan Watts, 2011] (www.factsanddetails.com).

  A lot of money is spent on infrastructure in China. An ambitious US$ 1.2 trillion public works program was announced in the late 1990s, towards efforts to keep economic growth rates high. It included the building of new bridges, roads, dams, railroads, power plants, port facilities and airports, all around the country. A fifth of all construction spending in China depends on public works projects. No other country in the world spends more, and devotes as much resources to infrastructure projects. (Ibid)

- Chinese sometimes achieve near-miraculous results by mobilizing massive labour forces. A thirty mile stretch of road, for example, had to be widened through rough mountainous terrain, between Chengdu and Guanxian. With the help of 200,000 labourers, it was completed in a week. In Xinjiang, a sandstorm once buried 350 miles of train track. Again with the help of thousands of labourers—and soldiers—it took only two days to clear it. (Ibid)

- The Chengdu-Kunming railway, which has 427 tunnels and 653 bridges, was built in 12 years. (Ibid)

- According to Elaine Kurtenbach, 2010, "China rolled out its fastest train yet and announced that the Three Gorges Dam, the world's biggest hydroelectric project, is now generating electricity at maximum capacity—engineering triumphs that signal the nation's growing ambitions, as its economy booms. The successes demonstrate how, after decades of acquiring technology from the west, Beijing has begun to push the limits of its new capabilities, setting the bar higher on mega-projects, as it seeks to promote the image of a powerful, modern China."

- "Still in the works: more nuclear power plants, a gargantuan project to pump river water from the fertile south to the arid north, and a US\$ 32.5 billion, 820-mile (1,300-kilometer) Beijing-to-Shanghai high-speed railway that is scheduled to open in 2012. Chinese companies are also vying for projects overseas, including in the US., which leads the world in freight railway technology, but has almost no high-speed rail expertise. That's a mark of how well and quickly the technology has been adopted by Chinese companies, who have traditionally only been able to compete on price in bidding for railway and other basic infrastructure projects in the developing world." [Ibid]

- China probably does a better job of executing big infrastructure, than almost any other country, anytime, anywhere, John Scales, in charge of transport issues for the World Bank's Beijing office, told the *New York Times*.

- After the global economic crisis, an economic stimulus package was approved in early 2009 by the Chinese government. The country built and expanded 35 airports, opened 557 kilometers of railways, including the world's fastest high-speed train, paved 98,000 kilometers of highways and picked up pace on subway projects from Shenyang in the north to Guangzhou in the south—all within a year.

- The Hangzhou Bay Bridge is the world's longest sea bridge. Opened in June 2007, it stretches 36 kilometers across Hangzhou Bay and connects Shanghai with Ningbo. It cost US$ 1.5 billion and has reduced the travel distance and time between Shanghai and Ningpo from 300 kilometers and four hours to 120 kilometers and 2½ hours.

- The longest cable-stayed bridge, the US$ 846 million Sutong Bridge, opened in the mid 2000s. Spanning the Yangtze River 300 kilometers upstream from Shanghai, it is 1,088 meters long.

- Oliver Pickup, 2010, "China has unveiled the world's longest sea bridge, which stretches a massive 26.4 miles (42.58 kilometers)—five miles further than the distance between Dover and Calais and longer than a marathon. The Qingdao Haiwan Bridge links the main urban area of Qingdao city, East China's Shandong province, with Huangdao district, straddling the Jiaozhou Bay sea areas.

- The longest bridge in the world, Danyang-Kunshan Grand Bridge, in China, is an astounding 102 miles in length. The next two longest bridges are also in China: the Tianjin Grand Bridge (a 71-mile-long rail bridge) and the Weinan Weihe Grand Bridge (a 50-mile-long rail bridge).

- In December 2009, China began construction of the world's longest sea bridge as part of a US$ 10 billion plan to rejuvenate the Pearl River Delta manufacturing area. The 31-mile-long bridge will link Hong Kong to the Chinese mainland and the gambling center of Macau in a giant Y-shape. [Peter

Foster, 2009]. Due for completion in 2016, the bridge will be designed to withstand tropical typhoons with winds up to 125mph, with almost 22 miles of its length, crossing the open sea. The project has been criticized as unnecessarily expensive, but officials said it was expected to create economic benefits of more than US$ 5.5 billion during its first 20 years. When completed, the six-lane expressway will link Hong Kong to Macau and the Pearl River Delta city of Zhuhai, cutting current road and ferry journey times from four-and-a-half hours to just 40 minutes. According to projections, more than 200 million vehicles a year will be using the bridge by 2020, carrying 170–220 million tons of freight. [Ibid]

The Bad

The world marvels at the lightening speed with which new roads and bridges appear on the Chinese landscape, with a minimum of bureaucratic fuss. What is less obvious is the social cost of ordinary people in terms of lost land and environmental problems, as these projects are rammed down the throats of citizens with little they can do to stop them. Some of these issues are as follows:

- China still relies as much on muscle and sweat, as machinery to complete its big jobs. In big cities, canals and building foundations are sometimes dug, not with bulldozers and earth movers, but by hand by men and women with buckets and poles balanced over their shoulders. On the Yangtze River, coal is delivered to barges by human chains of labourers with dirty coal piled high on their shoulders, and boats are pulled upstream and boulders are pulled uphill by workers harnessed to them by chains. (www.chinaknowledge.com).

- The Chengdu-Kunming railway, mentioned earlier in the article, was built by soldiers and prisoners who could be shot for shrinking from their duty on the job. Entire graveyards lying alongside the track are filled with men who died while constructing it.

- According to Elaine Kurtenbach (2010), many of these infrastructure initiatives have come at great human and environmental cost, and some have questioned whether the country fosters a sufficiently innovative spirit to compete at the next level. While tremendous growth has enabled China to build big, some wonder if it can build smart—and become a source of true innovation.

- Michael Clausecker, Director General of Unife, the Association of the European Rail Industry, said in an interview in 2009, "Science and technology research in the country tends to be heavily topdown, laden with a stifling government bureaucracy. Many of China's best scholars and scientists depart for greener pastures abroad, while other top minds are pushed into administrative roles, leaving them little time for research. Although China holds the patents on the technology, design and equipment used by the CRH380 train, some in industry question the degree to which China is justified in claiming the latest technology as its own. Everybody knows that a lot of the core technology is European."

- John Scales, mentioned earlier in the article, told the *New York Times* that things like environmental impact statements, and public hearings on controversial projects are easily avoided if the political will to do so is there.

- China has built its share of wasteful little-utilized infrastructure projects that hardly justify the money that was spent on them, Foremost among these, are airports that were built in remote places to promote tourism that never materialized. The airport in Libo, a small city of 166,000 in a beautiful mountainous region of poor Guizhou Province in southern China, cost US$ 57 million and has 50 full time workers, but only two flights a week. The airport was built to provide access to a forest reserves with spectacular canyons that was designated a UNESCO World Heritage site in 1996.

- Siphoning off money is reportedly a common practice. It is not unusual for a construction firm to win a contract to build a major project like a tunnel or bridge, and then subcontract the work to an unqualified firm, making a huge profit without lifting a shovel, or laying a beam. This seems so familiar to us in India.

The Ugly

There are some really dark secrets of this growth saga which are rarely brought out in the open, due to a highly restricted media and secretive government policies:

- Corruption, poor planning and shoddy construction have plagued infrastructure projects. A culture which puts premium on speed of completion, rather than quality of the work, fosters such practices (www.factsanddetails.com).
- Collapsing bridges, roads, dykes, buildings and dams are a serious problem in China. Dykes are filled with mud instead of concrete. Half finished skyscrapers lean dangerously to one side. Buildings lack proper foundations. Bridges are constructed with flawed designs. An estimated 33,000 dams and dykes need to be reinforced. Between 1949 and 1999, 3200 dams failed. (Ibid).
- In Chongqing alone, 1,600 people have died as a result of shoddy construction. Forty people died after falling 460 feet when the steel-and-concrete Rainbow Bridge over the Qijang River near Chongqing collapsed. An investigation uncovered faulty welding and US\$ 12,000 in bribes given to officials to overlook problems and allow the project to exceed its budget. (Ibid).
- The US\$ 52 million 1½-mile-long Zhaonoa Mountain bridge, built over the Yong River in Ningbo, was scheduled to open in

October, 1999. A month before its opening date, the bridge started to show slag and sway. Inspectors found large cracks caused by a design flaw due to wrong estimates of stress support in such a large structure. The bridge's opening was postponed and large sections of it had to be rebuilt. (Ibid).

- Road construction can be very shoddy. Sections of the Third Ring Road in Beijing collapsed in 2006 and again in 2007. Once, 18 days after a new 43-mile-long, US$ 43 million highway opened, huge potholes appeared and sections of the road buckled. Rubbish was found inside a barrier supposed to be made of solid concrete. Investigations uncovered widespread corruption, the use of substandard cement and slipshod workmanship. (Ibid).

- In August 2007, a bridge under construction collapsed in the tourist town of Fenghuang in Hunan Province, killing 47 people, most of them construction workers. (Ibid).

- A train crash near Wenzhou in eastern China that killed 40 people and injured 177 in July, 2011 brought attention to safety concerns about China's infrastructure. The train collision was one of several high-profile public transportation accidents in China around that time. A few days earlier, 41 people were killed when an overloaded bus caught fire in central Henan Province. Earlier in July, an escalator at a new subway station in Beijing collapsed, killing one person and injuring 28. The week before, four bridges collapsed in various Chinese cities. [Ian Johnson, 2011].

- Fear, that transparency and safety have become secondary to other concerns, was present in many postings on social networking and micro-blogging sites. One blogger in particular, posted an eloquent appeal for more care and caution in China's rapid development: "China, please stop your flying pace, wait for your people, wait for your soul, wait for your morality, wait for your conscience! Don't let the train run out off track, don't let the bridges collapse, don't let the roads become traps, don't let houses become ruins. Walk slowly, allowing every life to have freedom and dignity. No one should be left behind by our era."

- Explanations for the various bridge collapses tend to focus on the way in which the contracts to build them are distributed. Via virtually non-existent tender processes, local governments hand out projects to companies they themselves own. The work itself, however, is sub-contracted down an often bafflingly long chain of smaller companies, with bribes paid at each level, and successive layers of cash creamed from each strata. By the time the first shovel of cement enters the mixer, the actual budget that remains, allows for only the cheapest labour and often inferior materials.

Leo Lewis (2011) wrote in the *Times of London*, "Behind the accidents, say analysts, are features of the Chinese economy that could eventually become its undoing: huge corruption, praise of construction speed over build quality, and the failure to realize the gnawing, long-term cost of both these issues.

- In all this activity, it greatly helps to have a secretive planning bureaucracy and a government that tolerates little dissent. There was no consultation with the public on the new Beijing airport terminal. Nor was there any public debate about the construction of Beijing's third runway, notwithstanding the noise pollution already suffered by thousands of nearby residents. Beijing is now planning a second airport. The location is being considered in secret. Xu Li, an official at the Ministry of Communications' transport research institute, agrees that China's infrastructure expansion is not as restrained by rules, as it is in America. Once a plan is made, it is executed. "Democracy," she says, "sacrifices efficiency." (www.economist. com/node/10697210)

- An often heavy-handed approach to land appropriation also helps. For Beijing's airport expansion, 15 villages were flattened and their more than 10,000 residents resettled nearby. But, several of the former farmers told foreign media correspondents, that they were still barred from unemployment benefits and other welfare privileges of city dwellers, even though their farmland had been grabbed from them. One elderly man said that officials had threatened them with violence, if they refused to leave their villages. (Ibid).

- In China's biggest-ever urban protest against a transport-related project, thousands of Shanghai residents gathered outside the city government's headquarters in January to demand the cancellation of plans to extend a Maglev (magnetic levitation) train line through the city's main urban area. (Ibid).

- Complaints still abound about the way things work. Highways—both expressways and other intercity roads—are studded with traffic-slowing toll booths. China reportedly has 70 percent of the world's tolled roads, and its tolls are the highest in the world (using exchange rates adjusted according to currencies' purchasing power). To cut costs, trucks routinely overload. This helps to make the roads among the most dangerous in the world (89,000 deaths in 2006 by official reckoning; the actual number may be much higher). And it pushes up the costs of maintaining them. (Ibid).

Finally, looming over the whole scene is the increasingly troubling question of local government debt in China: economists are exercised about how far dangerously high levels of indebtedness have been masked, how many of the estimated 14.2 trillion yuan of loans to local government entities will turn bad, even if the global economy limps back to health, and how the world's second-biggest economy will react if the brakes are suddenly applied to fixed-asset investments, accounting for about 70 percent of gross domestic product. The concern is that in the country's unprecedented spree of infrastructure construction and other spending, local governments have already taken themselves close to the danger zone on debt: that line will inevitably be crossed if decades of shoddy work now require billions of yuan to put right. (Ibid)

All is certainly not well in the Dragon's Heaven.

Acknowledgement

I wish to express my heartfelt gratitude to my institute, the FORE School of Management, for providing me the opportunity to visit China and experience its culture, see its infrastructure and learn from Chinese faculty. This gave me the motivation to write this article.

References

Jonathan Watts, July 1, 2011, The Guardian.

www.factsanddetails.com/china.php?itemid=326&catid=13. accessed on 28.11.11 at 5.00 pm.

Acknowledgement: Jeffery Hays, 2008, www.factsanddetails.com/china

Elaine Kurtenbach, October 26, 2010, Associated Press.

Oliver Pickup, December 31, 2010, Daily Mail.

Peter Foster, December 15, 2009, The Telegraph.

www.chinaknowledge.com/.../CBGdetails.aspx accessed on 07.12.11 at 6.30 pm.

Ian Johnson, July 24, 2011, New York Times.

Leo Lewis, September 3, 2011, Times of London.

www.economist.com/node/10697210 accessed on 07.12.11 at 6.15 pm.

Higher Education Systems in China and India: Historical Perspectives and Challenges

Anupam Narula

FORE School of Management, New Delhi

E-mail: anupam@fsm.ac.in

ABSTRACT

China and India, which together have a third of the world's population, and are two of the most rapidly growing economies, are awakening to the significance of higher education for technological development, and for the global knowledge economy. China has made considerable progress with its top institutions, and India has shown in technical education with the Indian Institutes of Technology and in management with the Indian Institutes of Management and a few other institutions that high standards are possible. Yet, the problem of poor quality, and the related issues of whether the graduates are qualified for the job market remain.

This article highlights the development of the higher education system in the two countries from the very beginning, and the main challenge of access and equity being faced by both countries.

Keywords: *Chinese Higher Education System, Indian Higher Education System, Western Academic Model, Educational Reforms, Restructuring, Gross Enrolment Ratio, Scientific Technology Parks. Higher Education Access, Mass Access and Equity.*

"Wisdom is knowing what to do next, skill is knowing how to do it and virtue is doing it"

—David Starr Jordan

"All who have meditated on the art of governing mankind have been convinced that the fate of empires depends on the education of youth".

—*Aristotle*

"The empires of the future will be empires of the mind. With great power comes great responsibility".

—*Winston Churchill*

Introduction

China and India, which together have a third of the world's population, and are two of the most rapidly growing economies, are awakening to the significance of higher education for technological development, and for the global knowledge economy. The economic realities of China and India's rapid growth are affecting the world, from increased demand for natural resources to their roles as exporters of products of all kinds, a pattern that will continue regardless of the current economic slowdown. A growing impact of these countries is in higher education; their higher education systems are already among the world's largest; and they are major exporters of students to other countries. This trend is likely to grow in the future, as these countries expand and improve their higher education systems. Although the booms of China and India have been fuelled in the main by cheap labour and inexpensive low-end manufacturing, the situation is changing, and the economic future of both countries depends on a better-educated workforce. Universities are central in the race to provide respective workforces with skills to make them competitive in the global knowledge system.

Both countries realize that higher education is the key to development and recognize the necessity to expand their higher education systems and to build some world-class research universities at the top of a differentiated system. In 2006, India educated approximately 12 percent of its university-age population, while China enrolled about 22 percent (UIS, 2009). China is now number one in enrolments, with more than 25 million. India's 13 million enrolment ranks third. Both countries have been expanding rapidly in recent years. Since the early 1990s, China's postsecondary enrolments have grown from 5 million to 25 million in 2006, while India has expanded from 5 million to 13 million by 2006 (Agarwal, 2009; OECD, 2007b). Perhaps, one-third of the world's 140 million postsecondary students are in Chinese and Indian institutions of higher education.

Significant quality problems exist in less-selective colleges and universities in both countries. Many of India's impressive number of engineering graduates, up to 75 percent according to a McKinsey report, are too poorly educated to function effectively in the economy, without additional on-the-job training (Jha, 2009; Surowiecki, 2007). Part of China's growing problem of graduate unemployment is related to the qualifications of some students.

Higher education comprises a policy priority in both countries. China has for almost two decades been engaged in a significant upgrade in the quality of its top universities, as well as in a major expansion of enrolments in all higher education sectors. While India has for decades recognised the importance of expanding higher education access and improving quality, only quite recently have significant resources been allocated, with the Knowledge Commission's higher education recommendations of 2006, and more recent government commitments (Tilak, 2007). Current plans, for example, call for expanding the number of top-tier higher education institutions (Agarwal, 2009).

Envisioning higher education prospects for China and India for two decades, or more is highly complex. Basic stability and consistent policy orientations for higher education, as seen from today's perspective, cannot be predicted with great certainty into the coming decades for either country. In a way, China today may be seen as too stable, while India as perhaps overly unstable. India's relatively open political system may permit it more flexibility in coping with adversity, but it could fail to produce practical solutions, or imaginative plans to improve higher education. China's state planning system has developed higher education impressively, especially at the top of the system, but may lack flexibility. Both may be struck by internal forces, or regional and global changes more profoundly than many parts of the world. The past shows that China is capable of dramatic and sometimes unpredictable policy shifts. India, constantly debating new directions, changes gradually and often without clear planning.

The future of higher education policy in both countries depends to a significant degree on several factors. Demand relates to the continuing expansion of the middle class, that has the resources to pay tuition and other fees and educational qualifications for admission. Other population groups have an interest in higher education access as well, but the middle class is the largest force, has dramatically expanded in recent years, and is likely to continue to grow. While estimates vary considerably, many experts agree that the Indian middle class now number more than 50 million, and China's is similarly large. Some estimates (for example by McKinsey Global Institute) predict that by 2025, each country will have a middle class of perhaps 500 million. A significant number of these large groups will demand access to higher education, creating huge strains on the system. Government policy regarding funding higher education and supporting research universities and the elite sector of the system, is a key factor shaping higher education prospects. As both countries join the ranks of the world's major economies, they will recognize the importance of world-class universities, so as to compete globally. China has already moved to create and sustain an elite academic sector. India is beginning to grapple with this issue.

A Historical Sketch

For higher education systems, history plays a role in the present. For both China and India, the academic past has created difficult and complex results for the present and likely for the future. In common with all of the world's higher education systems, both inherited the western academic model (Ben-David and Zloczower, 1962). Both countries have largely not taken advantage of their extraordinarily rich indigenous intellectual and academic traditions. China, after all, in the beginning of the 20th century, abolished the civil service examination system, and established a modern school system based on Western models. In 1922, it adopted the American model, and this dominated the Chinese higher education system until 1949. By then China had 205 higher education institutions: 124 public universities, 21 missionary-run universities and 60 private universities and colleges, mostly concentrated on the east coast and in Beijing and a few other large cities and with a total enrolment of 116,504 students. In 1952, all the higher education institutions, including the 60 private institutions, were brought under the jurisdiction of the Communist government, and the Soviet model was adopted to restructure the China's higher education system, in order to serve the manpower needs for building a socialist China. After this structural change, China's higher education, as part of a centrally planned economy, became departmentalized, segmented and overspecialized; teaching was separated from research. Academic freedom became limited, and the emergence of an effective academic profession got hindered.

In 1958, China made its first attempt to expand the higher education sector, in order to make possible an ambitious economic growth plan, the so-called Great Leap Forward for Socialist Construction. From 1958 to 1960, the number of universities and colleges, as well as student enrolments, increased drastically. More than 100 new higher education institutions were established, and total enrolments increased to 961,623 in 1960 from 441,181 in

1957. Yet, this attempt to expand higher education failed, along with the failure of the Great Leap Forward. The government then had to readjust the higher education development policy, and the number of higher education institutions was reduced to 407 in 1963 from 1,289. However, this experience did not change the dominance of the Soviet model: the higher education sector was still part of the planned economy; the government was entirely responsible for the costs of higher education and for graduate job assignment. After 1978, with the end of the Cultural Revolution of 1966–76, China restored its higher education system, and started educational reforms along with a move to a market-oriented socialist economy. In 1985, the central government announced its reform plan, and embarked upon a decentralization process, which gave the local government and higher education institutions more autonomy. A university system was then required to have multiple functions: teaching, research, business and social services. In 1993, the government launched further reform measures to increase accessibility to higher education, and a "user-pays" system was implemented, along with fundamental changes in the job assignment system.

In the context of globalization and continued economic reforms, Chinese higher education in the 1990s underwent reforms similar to those in other parts of the world: that is, the marketization of higher education, where greater emphasis was placed on efficiency, competition and accountability. As well as the "user-pays" system of student fees in tertiary education, and changes in the graduate job assignment system, nongovernment-supported institutions of higher education began to emerge for the first time since 1949. Until 1999, Chinese higher education expanded gradually. From 1978 to 1996, tertiary student enrolment increased from 0.86 to 0.9658 million. In 1997, after the implementation of the fee-charging system nationwide, regular universities' enrolments increased to 1.04 million; in 1998 the enrolment number reached

1.0836 million. Then, in 1999, the government decided to accelerate the pace of expansion, and enrolments in higher education institutions increased dramatically. Regular universities' enrolment was planned to increase to 1.537 million from 1.08 million in 1998, an increase of 41.7 percent; yet, the actual enrolment number reached 1.59 million, an increase of 47.4 percent. The total enrolment for all types of higher education institutes in 1999 was over 2.7 million. Reforms picked up the pace in 2000, with the state aiming to complete the reform of 200 universities operating under China's ministries, and start 15 university-based scientific technology parks. From 2002 to 2005, higher education institutions increased from 2000 to 4000, and student enrollments increased to 15 million in 2005 from 11.26 million in 2002. In a country of 1.3 billion people, the higher education system does not meet the needs of 85 percent of the college-aged population. In recent years, 10 universities have been targeted by the Chinese government to become "world-class"—including *Peking* and *Tsinghua* universities. Universities are once again required to be centers of teaching and research, and internationally oriented programs constitute an increasing proportion of the curriculum.

India was a British colony for more than two centuries, ending with independence in 1947, and this experience shaped higher education and continues to influence it. The British did not give much support to higher education in their colonies. Higher education first expanded mainly due to the initiative of the growing middle class in the mid-19th century, and recognition by the British that an educated civil service was needed to administer India. In 1857, the first universities were founded in Calcutta, Bombay, and Madras. The focus in these universities was on creating aristocratic, English educated Indian workers for the civil services, and strengthening the foundation of British rule in India. The industrialist Jamsetji Tata envisioned an unique institution for scientific research and study and setup the Indian Institute of

Science, Bangalore in 1911. Later on, 20 universities like the B.H.U., MGKVP, and AMU also came into existence, along with some of the other universities in the country. With Nehru's vision, India's new higher education institutes such as lITs, IIMs and AIIMS were established after independence.

However, the academic system remained quite small, and has witnessed many fold increase in institutional capacity since independence. From 1950 to 2008, the number of universities, deemed universities and institutions of national importance have increased from 20 to about 440, colleges from 500 to 20,677 and teachers from 15,000 to nearly 5.05 lakhs. Consequently, the enrolment of students have increased from a mere 1.00 lakh in 1950 to over 115 lakhs. The enrolment ratio at the aggregate level (GER) in higher education, based on selected educational statistics (2007–08) comes to around 11 percent of the eligible population for higher education i.e. 18–23 year age group youth. The government has embarked on reforms in higher education so early in its terms is indeed creditable. But, the growth is comparatively much faster in the last two years. The number of universities, deemed universities and colleges in 2008 was 440 and 20,667 respectively, which increased to 519 universities and 25,951 colleges in 2010. GER in higher education increased to 13 percent, but to make use of the new opportunities to achieve equity in access along with quality of institutions in respect of quality teachers, infrastructure and funding, research and industry interface etc., is a big challenge for India.

Challenges of Access and Equity

The population of China exceeded 1.3 billion and that of India 1.1 billion in 2007 (World Bank 2008). One of the greatest challenges to higher education in both countries consists of providing access to the growing segments of the population demanding post-secondary education. A related issue is providing equity to population groups underrepresented in the student population. At present, India is still at the "elite" stage of access, with 12 percent higher education gross enrolment ratio in 2006, up from 6 percent in 1991 (World Bank, 2008a). The government has recognised the need to expand access from 10 percent (Trow, 2006) to 15 percent of the age cohort during the 11th Five-Year Plan (2007–12) and to 21 percent by the end of the following plan, in 2017. This expansion would be the largest in India's history, and will require a dramatic growth in institutions as well as expenditure. China, already at a 22 percent participation level in 2006 against 3 percent in 1991 (World Bank, 2008a), is approaching mass access. It builds from a higher base, but significant expansion will take place as well. In 2005, the Minister of Education indicated that the participation rate would be 40 percent by 2020. Indeed, the majority of the world's enrolment growth in the coming two decades will take place in just these two countries (Kapur and Crowley, 2008).

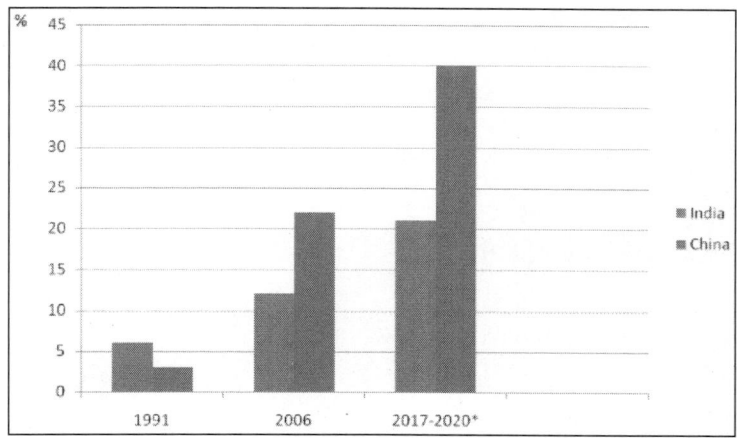

Fig. 1: Higher Education Participation in China and India (gross enrolment ratio 1991–2006, official targets for 2017 and 2020)

*official Targets.

Sources: World Bank (2008a); Kapur and Crowley (2008); Trow (2006).

Both countries recognize the need to focus more on postsecondary education, and they have seen dramatic expansion in the past decade, and plan on continued growth in the coming decades. A variety of strategies are evident, and they are similar in both countries. The private sector is a major source of "demand absorption." The countries have permitted the continuing expansion of private institutions, although both are uncertain about the conditions under which the private sector should function.

Not the same issue as access, equity involves higher education for population groups that may be underrepresented in the system and includes, depending on the country or region, gender and socio-economic inequalities, rural and urban disparities, and ethnic or other minority groups. The urban and rural divide, both in China and India is immense, with implications for access and equity. In common with many developing countries, a majority of the population lives in rural areas. Even with the dramatic urbanization in both countries, a substantial majority of the population is still rural, where income, literacy, access to education at all levels, life expectancy, and quality of life measures are all lower than for the urban areas. Access to higher education is dramatically lower, and quality tends to be lower as well.

In higher education, as in other aspects of society and the economy, the disparity between the affluent coastal areas and the vast interior is significant. Rates of access to higher education in western China are significantly lower than in the coastal areas such as Guangdong, Zhejiang, Jiangsu and Fujian, and the large cities like Shanghai, Beijing and Shenzhen. Fewer data are available concerning access rates for China's minority groups, and disparities according to gender or social class. However, major inequalities persist. The rapid economic growth over the past 20 years has actually widened the gaps between the "haves" and "have not's" in society. For instance, in 1990 per capita GDP in Shanghai was 7.3 times higher than that in Guizhou; in 1998 it was 12.1 times higher; in 1999 it was 12.46 times higher. It is possible that the continued prosperity in the high growth regions of the country may raise inequalities, although much of the data are unavailable.

The most controversial issues in Indian higher education, include an array of policies aimed at improving access and equity for tribal groups, lower castes, and *dalits*. Policies relating to what in India is called "positive discrimination" are politically charged. Since independence in 1947, positive discrimination, also called reservations, throughout the public employment system and in higher education in India, has meant that *dalits* and some additional lower castes (known as Other Backward Castes) and tribal groups have proportions of seats in colleges and universities, positions in the civil service, and some other sectors reserved for them. This means that postsecondary institutions are required to hire and enrol, a fixed percentage of these groups—*almost half of the total*. Positive discrimination has been claimed as largely ineffective in raising the status of the groups it is intended to help, and a mistaken social policy in a meritocratic society (Mahajan, 2007). At the same time, court orders have expanded the scope of the "reservation" system to institutions, such as the Indian Institutes of Technology, where it was not fully in place before, but has renewed the debate about the policy in general.

Conclusion

China and India are already major global forces in higher education (Altbach 2007). As they move towards international norms of access to higher education, China and India could together be expected to account for over half of the global increase in student numbers. It is certain that both are two of the world's largest academic systems, but it is less clear that these systems will be globally competitive.

China and India exhibit a great need for better regulation, as well as more academic qualifications, teaching experience, and understanding of social changes and technology. To this end, top universities and institutions should function as centers of excellence that serve as a model for all other institutes. A helpful model involved "twinning" of poorer institutes with model institutes to provide equipment, curricula, and faculty development.

As noted, China has made considerable progress with its top institutions, and India has illustrated with the Indian Institutes of Technology and IIMs that high standards are possible. Yet, the overall excellence and effectiveness of the systems themselves need improvement. The problem of quality, and the related issues of whether graduates are qualified for the labour market, remains in question. Generally, the overall standards tend to decline in an academic system that is expanding dramatically. There is also an issue of funding and equity. The cost of adding facilities is high. Both countries will be required to provide significant additional financial support for higher education over the coming decades. Part of the expansion will depend on the continued growth of the private sector, and on distance education. The countries have yet to fully integrate the private higher education sector into the higher education system, or to create appropriate regulatory and quality assurance frameworks for the private sector. Some uncertainties about the private sector continue. In the coming years, the private sector must be integrated into the mainstream, if the expansion is to be fully accomplished.

Also, there are concerns about the mindset of students produced by Chinese and Indian institutions. Cheating is widespread and tolerated, within a reasonable level. Many corporations feel the quality of rote memorization instilled in Chinese and Indian students, serves as a detriment to creative thinking and the lack of real-world experience during the formative years, which negatively impacts students' ability to adapt to the global business environment easily. These issues will need to be addressed in the coming years, if China and India aims, to continue their drive for excellence.

References

Figures and information are from Surveys of the Educational Reform and Development in China (Ministry of Education, 1996, 1997, 1998).

Figures cited here come from Min Weifang (2004), "Historical perspectives and contemporary challenges: the case of Chinese universities",

For a discussion of China's educational reform in the 1990s, see Limin Bai, "The metamorphosis of China's higher education in the 1990s", in Keith Sullivan (ed.), "Education and Change in the Pacific Rim, Meeting the Challenges", *Oxfordshire, UK: Triangle Books* (1998), pp. 241–265.

http://en.wikipedia.org/wiki/Higher_education_in_China.

http://www.tc.columbia.edu/centers/coce/publications.htm#(c).

Kang Ning, "On education policy and the creating of a new system", in China's Educational Policy, Beijing, 2000, pp. 9–10; Surveys of the Educational Reform and Development in China (Ministry of Education, 1999).

Li Ning (1999), "Economy maintains steady growth", in *Beijing Review*, Vol. 42, No. 32, p. 20.

OECD (2004), "Quality and Recognition in Higher Education: The Cross-border Challenge", OECD Publishing, Paris.

OECD (2005), "Guidelines for Quality Provision in Cross-border Higher Education", OECD Publishing, Paris,

OECD (2008), "Tertiary Education for the Knowledge Society", OECD Thematic Review of Tertiary Education: Synthesis Report Volume 2 Assuring and Improving Quality, OECD Publishing, Paris.

Policy Futures in Education (2004), "Higher education in China today", Vol. 2, No. 1 p. 142.

Salmi, J. (2000), "Tertiary Education in the 21st century: Challenges and Opportunities", Washington DC: World Bank.

Surveys of the Educational Reform and Development in China; Ministry of Education, 1998.

Tang Min, chief economist of the Asian Development Bank Mission in China, proposed using higher education.

The figures and information are from Regions and Development; Beijing, 2004 at http://www.cas.cn/html/books/061BG/d1/xbkf04.htm)

www.oecd.org/dataoecd/27/51/35779480.pdf.

Xi Mi, "Market confronts education reform", *Beijing Review*, Vol. 42, No. 44 (1999), p. 21.

Commercial Banking in Chindia - China and India

Vinay Dutta

FORE School of Management, New Delhi

E-mail: vinay@fsm.ac.in

ABSTRACT

Operations and performance of commercial banks in China and India engage the attention of all globally, as both are emerging economies and both have introduced significant banking sector reforms in the recent past. This article examines the operations and performance of commercial banks operating in China and India during the period 2010–2011 on select parameters such as changes in ownership patterns, structure and size, and operational performance in the context of the continuing banking sector reforms in these countries. The article also details the major challenges that Chinese and Indian commercial banks may face in coming times due to the adverse global financial environment, as well as high inflation prevailing in these economies.

Keywords: Commercial Banks, Emerging Economies, Banking Sector Reforms, Bank Performance.

Introduction

A robust banking system is a pre-requisite for a well-functioning economy. Banking systems in China and India are no exception, and plays an important role in accelerating the process of growth in their respective economies. Though banking systems differ from country to country, as do their national state of affairs (*Refer* Table 1 Economy Overview), banking systems in China and India have undergone remarkable changes over the last few decades, and the process of transformation is continuing. This article examines commercial banking systems in China and India on parameters such as ownership, size, operations and performance etc in the context of banking sector reforms and identifies the challenges ahead.

Table 1: Economy Overview

Parameters	China	India
Region	East Asia and Pacific	South Asia
Population	1,338,300,000	1,170,938,000
GNI per capita (USUS$)	4260	1340
DB 2012 rank	91	132
DB 2011 rank	87	139
Gross Domestic Product (USUS$ billion December 2010)	5879[#] (9.48% of the world economy)	1729[#] (2.79% of the world economy)
Commercial banks share of GDP (2010)	186.3[+]	

Source: Doing Business—The World Bank/IFC 2012—Economy Profile: China/India.
[#] China GDP (http://www.tradingeconomics.com/china/gdp and India GDP (http://www.tradingeconomics.com/india/gdp)
[+] IMF Country Report No. 11/321, Nov. 2011.

Commercial Banks

Commercial banks are essential to most of us, because these institutions accepts deposits, make loans, provide payments and a settlement framework, and offers a variety of related financial services in an economy. Commercial banks create money and the creation of money assumes special significance in the context of emerging economies like China and India, as performance of banks have a direct bearing on their economic growth. Commercial banking as an industry in these economies is rapidly transforming, to keep pace with economic reforms taking place within China and

India and across the globe. Another reason for change in the banking sector in China and India, is because commercial banking systems in these economies are gradually aligning with that of the developed world. As much of the rest of the world continues to struggle in the aftermath of the recent financial debacle, it is interesting to study organizational issues, operations, performance of commercial banks in China and India and how these institutions are shaping up to embrace global challenges.

Structure and Ownership of Commercial Banks

China boasts of some of the biggest banks in the world, and these banks are in a commanding position to capitalise on China's growing stature on the world stage. Chinese commercial banks primarily consist of large commercial banks (LCBs), nation-wide joint-stock commercial banks (JSCBs) which are partially owned by the local government and state owned enterprises, and in some cases by the corporate sector, city commercial banks (with business restricted to the home city), rural commercial banks and foreign banks. LCBs were originally established to serve different economic sectors and to extend loans for policy objectives. In 1994, LCBs were re-organised as commercial banks. These banks are now in direct competition with each other. (*Refer,* Table 2, Banks in China as at end of 2010).

Table 2: Banks in China as at end of 2010

Type of Institutions	Number of Banks
Large Commercial Banks	5
Joint-Stock Commercial Banks	12
City Commercial Banks	147
Rural Commercial Banks	85
Foreign Banks	40

Source: Appendix 8–15, CBRC-2010 Annual Report.

As the principal stakeholder, the state appoints senior management in all major banks. In the absence of an explicit deposit insurance system and a resolution framework, the state also implicitly insures all deposits. The direct and indirect remote control by the state in almost all policy and operational areas concerning Chinese commercial banks, impacts the efficacy of market discipline and corporate governance. To bring in institutional reforms, the China Banking Regulatory Commission (CBRC) has taken several initiatives to mobilize participation of private capital in the banking sector. Accordingly, a series of policies were issued to facilitate private capital's participation in various activities, ranging from state-owned commercial banks' reforms and public listings, to small- and medium-sized commercial banks' equity optimization, and to rural credit cooperatives' restructuring. With the IPOs of the Agricultural Bank of China (ABC) in 2010, all five LCBs have completed their public listings, and thereby transformed from wholly state-owned commercial banks to public banks, with a more diversified shareholding structure. At the same time, these banks have continuously improved their corporate governance as well as operational and management efficiency. In 2010, the five banks replenished their capital base by issuing subordinated debts, and actively prepared for the implementation of Basel II and Basel III. It is expected that private capital in the banking sector will benefit from a diversified ownership structure, will facilitate provision of customized products and services, and result in better disclosures and capital management.

Commercial banking institutions in India commonly referred to as scheduled commercial banks (SCBs-SCBs in India constitute those banks which have been included in the Second Schedule of the Reserve Bank of India (RBI) Act, 1934. RBI in turn includes only those banks in this schedule which satisfy the criteria laid down vide section 42(6) (a) of the Act) comprise of public sector banks (nationalised banks and the State Bank group), private sector banks (old and newly established after opening up of the banking sector in 1990), regional rural banks and foreign banks (Refer, Table 3, Banks in India as at end of March 2011).

Table 3: Banks in India as at end of March 2011

Type of Institutions	Number of Banks
Public Sector Banks (these include State Bank of India, its five associates, 19 nationalised banks and IDBI Bank Ltd.)	26
Private Sector Banks (7 new private sector banks and 14 old private sector banks)	21
Regional Rural Banks	82
Foreign banks	36

Source: RBI Report on Trend and Progress of Banking in India 2010–11.

Unlike China, deposit insurance constitutes an important element in preventing any runs on the banks in India due to unforeseen events. The Deposit Insurance and Credit Guarantee Corporation (DICGC), a wholly owned subsidiary of the Reserve Bank of India, provides deposit insurance coverage at ₹ 1 lakh per depositor per bank. At the current level, the insurance cover works out to 1.63 times per capita GDP as on 31 March, 2011 as against the international benchmark of around 1 to 2 times per capita GDP prior to the financial crisis.

Government shareholding in public sector banks ranged roughly between 57 percent and 85 percent in 2010–11, though the minimum statutory requirement is 51 percent. While, twelve out of 21 public sector banks had less than ten percent foreign shareholding in 2010–11, the rest had less than 20 percent foreign shareholding, while all the new private banks had a foreign shareholding of more than 30 percent against 74 percent, the regulatory maximum prescribed by the Reserve Bank of India. For further opening up of the banking sector, the Reserve Bank is in the process of finalizing guidelines in consultation with the

Government of India on entry of new banks in the private sector in India.

Performance of Commercial Banks

Both the Chinese and Indian banking sectors performed better in 2010–11 despite the challenging economic environment. Banks in China and India recorded higher growth in 2010–11 as compared to their performance during the last year. As of end 2010, total assets and total liabilities of Chinese banking institutions grew by 19.9 percent and 19.2 percent on a year-on-year basis. During 2010–11, Indian banks deposits and advances grew at 18.3 percent and 22.9 percent. In terms of capital adequacy (ratio of capital to risk weighted assets), return on assets (net profits/average total assets), return on equity (net profits/average total equity), non-performing loans and asset base and non performing loans (assets) too, Chinese and Indian Banks displayed improvement (*Refer.* Table 4 Capital Adequacy Ratio, Return on Assets, Return on Equity and Non-Performing Loans of Chinese/Indian SCBs). It is evident from the table, that the capital adequacy ratio (ratio of capital to risk weighted assets of the commercial banks) of Chinese and Indian banks is well above the stipulated norms. This implies that, in the short to medium terms, banks are not constrained by capital in extending credit, unless the quality of loan portfolio deteriorates substantially. Research reports compiled by the Asian Banker in October 2011 states that 98 Chinese banks with US$ 10,756 billion in assets and US$ 112.2 billion in net profits and 49 Indian banks with assets totaling US$ 1,334 billion and net profits totaling US$ 12.6 billion ranked in the 2011–2012 AB500. However, performance of commercial banks in these economies was conditioned by the dynamics of the growth-inflation trade-off. There is apprehension that a Chinese subprime lending crisis and inflation may cool down Chinese banks' growth engines. Likewise, escalating interest rates and bad loans may weaken the financial growth of banks in

India, and impact their capital adequacy ratios, return on assets and return on equity downward.

Table 4: Capital Adequacy Ratio, Return on Assets, Return on Equity and Non-performing Loans of Chinese and Indian SCBs

(percent)

Commercial Banks/All SCBs	China		India	
	End 2009	End 2010	2009– 10	2010– 11
Capital Adequacy Ratio	11.0	12.2	14.5*	14.2*
Return on Asset	1.0	1.1	1.05	1.10
Return on Equity	18.0	19.2	14.31	14.96
Non-performing Loans+	1.6	1.1	2.25	2.39

Source: Appendix 8–6, 8–9 and 8–13, CBRC-2010 Annual Report.

Source: RBI Report on Trend and Progress of Banking in India 2010–11/* As per Basel II /+NPAs to gross advances ratio.

Challenges Ahead

Among the emerging economies, China and India's commercial banks have exhibited growth in the size of the asset base, level of deposits and increasing capital patterns and decreasing non-performing loans on a year on year basis at a time when the banking sector in most advanced economies were in a phase of contraction following the financial mess. The growth in banks assets and credit, have remained at a high level in 2010. The strong growth environment does lead to an improved corporate credit profile, but both Chinese and Indian banks have high exposure to vulnerable sectors such as commercial real estate and the export oriented sectors. Performance of China's and India's banking system will also rest on what happens with inflation, and the magnitude of policy tightening. In the high inflation/high interest rate scenario and tightening in credit, the impact on the corporate and banking sectors will likely be damaging. More aggressive policy moves, increasing borrowing costs and more limited access to credit, could begin to erode the performance of Chinese/Indian corporates, in turn sparking a rise in corporate loan delinquencies and deterioration in bank financials. Further, due to ensuing European financial crisis and sluggish economic growth in the US, the Chinese and Indian commercial banks will not only see a slowdown in credit growth, but also rising possibilities of deterioration in asset quality, on the back of weakening of the repayment capacities of borrowers in general. The tight interest rate environment, and increasing delinquencies may also affect the profit prospects of commercial banks in 2011–12. Besides, the adverse economic environment and resultant weakening asset quality, concerns have been raised on the slow pace of financial inclusion, weak corporate governance mechanisms, and slow adoption of modern operational concepts, lack of effective risk management and business procedures practiced by Chinese and Indian banks.

In conclusion, it is recommended that both Chinese and Indian commercial banks should continue to innovate and transform their respective banking systems through strengthening of the financial inclusion process, adoption of modern operational concepts and developmental strategies, such as shifting from chasing business volume and scale, to improving the quality of customer service, paying attention to maximization of shareholder value, retaining a competitive edge, establishing a modern corporate governance framework, and improving risk management capabilities.

References

China Banking Regulatory Commission-2010 Annual Report.

IMF Country Report No. 11/321, People's Republic of China: Financial System Stability Assessment, November 2011.

Report on Trend and Progress of Banking in India 2010–11.

The Asian Banker Research Note, China: Fears of possible credit risk and inflation temper booming growth, October 05, 2011.

The Asian Banker Research Note, India: Mounting interest rates, bad loans dim outlook, October 11, 2011.

Global Crisis Response and Its Implications: India *vs* China

Mathew Joseph

FORE School of Management, New Delhi

E-mail: mathew.joseph@fsm.ac.in

ABSTRACT

The stimulus measures introduced in China to combat the global crisis helped to raise the investment rate in the economy, whereas Indian measures raised the consumption rate. As a result, the productive capacity of the economy rose in China, whereas it declined in India during the crisis. A large part of the stimulus spending was financed by banks in China, while it was financed by the government budget in India. This resulted in a weakening of the financial sector in China, while in India that led to the weakening of the fiscal position.

Keywords: Fiscal Stimulus, Global Crisis Impact, India, China.

Introduction

More than four years after the outbreak of the global financial crisis in 2008, countries are yet to recover fully, and the crisis in the euro-zone countries has prolonged the agony. Although the swift policy measures taken by governments, averted the danger of nations tipping into a depression, new problems have arisen from the way in which countries responded to the global crisis. Basically, all nations took recourse to ultra loose fiscal and monetary policies to combat the impact of the global crisis. However, the degree and manner in which governments operated the new policy differed. The after effects also varied, depending on the degree and manner of the administration of the loose macro policy. In this context, it would be interesting to examine how China and India responded to the global crisis, and what are the implications of those responses.

Chinese Policy Response

The Chinese economy had been growing rapidly before the crisis, and its GDP growth crossed 14 percent in 2007 (Table 1). The global crisis surely hit the economy hard, and the growth dropped to 9.6 percent in 2008 and 9.2 percent in 2009, before recovering to 10.4 percent in 2010. A predominantly export-dependent economy, the collapse in export growth—the growth in exports volume declined to 8.4 percent in 2008 from 19.8 percent in 2007, and turned negative −10.3 percent in 2009—triggered the sharp decline in GDP growth during the crisis.

The Chinese government implemented a policy package consisting of a mix of macroeconomic and industrial policy measures. A stimulus package of 4 trillion Yuan of public expenditure was announced in November, 2008. The structure of spending as indicated by the National Development and Reforms Commission, had mostly been towards economic and social infrastructure—transportation network, earthquake reconstruction, rural infrastructure, urban housing, health and education. The structure of financing the package had been prescribed as (i) central government financing (about 25 percent of total) in the form of direct grants, interest rate subsidies and spending on central government projects, (ii) central government support for financing local projects, and (iii) bank lending for local government projects. Along with the expansionary fiscal policy, monetary policy was also loosened in November, 2008 by cutting down interest rates to a historical low level, lowering bank reserve ratio requirements and abolishing the quota control on lending by commercial banks. Besides these, other stimulus measures included tax reductions, VAT reform, business tax cuts, increase in export rebate rates, and raising the threshold of individual income taxes (Zhang, Liqing, 2009).

Table 1: Crisis and After—Select Economic Indicators of China

	2005	*2006*	*2007*	*2008*	*2009*	*2010*	*2011*
Gross domestic product, constant prices, % change	11.3	12.7	14.2	9.6	9.2	10.4	9.2
Total investment, % of GDP	42.1	43.0	41.7	44.0	48.2	47.7	48.3
Gross national savings, % of GDP	48.0	51.6	51.9	53.2	53.5	52.9	51.0
General government revenue, % of GDP	17.2	18.2	19.8	19.7	20.0	20.2	22.3
General government total expenditure, % of GDP	18.6	18.9	18.9	20.0	23.1	22.5	23.6
General government net lending/borrowing, % of GDP	−1.4	−0.7	0.9	−0.4	−3.1	−2.3	−1.2
Inflation, average consumer prices, % change	1.8	1.5	4.8	5.9	−0.7	3.3	5.4
Volume of imports of goods and services, % change	13.4	16.0	13.9	3.7	4.2	20.1	9.5
Volume of exports of goods and services, % change	23.6	23.9	19.8	8.4	−10.3	28.4	8.2
Current account balance, % of GDP	5.9	8.6	10.1	9.1	5.2	5.1	2.8

Source: International Monetary Fund, World Economic Outlook Database, April 2012.

An important feature of the Chinese government's policy measures has been that they helped in protecting and raising further the high savings and investment levels in the economy during the crisis period (Chart 1). China's savings rate had been in the range of 48–51.9 percent of GDP during 2005–2007, and the rate rose to 53.2 percent in 2008 and further to 53.5 percent in 2009.

Chart 1: Savings and Investments in China, 2005–2011

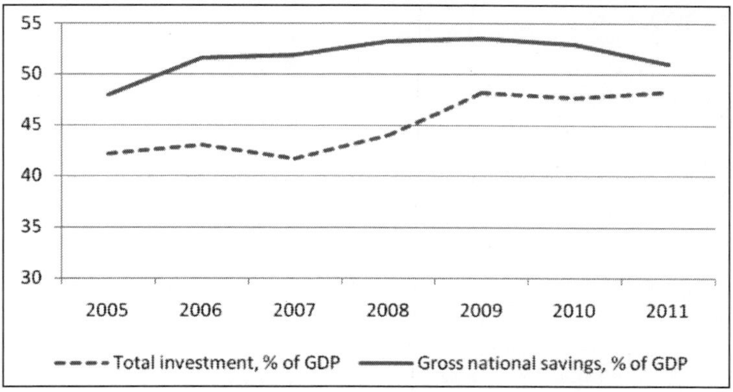

Source: IMF, World Economic Outlook Database, April 2012.

Gross investment had been around 41.7–43 percent of GDP during 2005–2007, and it increased to 44 percent in 2008, and further to 48.2 percent in 2009 (Table 1). Thus, the fiscal and monetary stimulus administered by the Chinese authorities, boosted savings and investments in the economy. Government expenditure did go up from 18.9 percent of GDP in 2007 to 20 percent and 23.1 percent in 2008 and 2009 respectively. China had a marginal fiscal surplus of 0.9 percent of GDP in 2007. That turned into a deficit of 0.4 percent of GDP, and higher deficit of 3.1 percent of GDP in 2009.

Indian Policy Response

It is interesting to note that the Indian policy response began much before the impact of the global crisis got transmitted to the economy. Early in fiscal year 2008–09, certain populist measures were undertaken, such as salary hike for the government staff, debt waiver for farmers, additional expenditure for the rural employment scheme, and duty reductions on petroleum products. As the crisis began to hit the economy, the central government announced three successive fiscal stimulus packages one in December 2008, the second in early 2009 and the last in early March 2009. These included: across-the-board central duty reductions by 4 percentage points; additional plan spending of ₹ 200 billion; additional borrowings by state governments of ₹ 300 billion for plan expenditure; assistance to certain export industries in the form of interest rate subsidy on export finance, refund of excise duties/central sales tax, and other export incentives; and a two percentage-point reduction in central excise and service tax. The total fiscal burden for these packages amounted to only 1.8 percent of GDP. The earlier populist measures involved much more (Joseph, Mathew, 2009).

Other government steps included relaxation of external commercial borrowing rules, raising the cap on FII investments in debt, and permission given to the India Infrastructure Financing Company Limited (IIFCL) in floating tax-free bonds for infrastructure funding. The Reserve Bank of India (RBI) acted aggressively from mid-September 2008, to ease the liquidity situation by a series of rate cutting and liquidity injecting measures until April 2009.

India also had been growing very fast before the crisis, and the GDP growth rate touched 10 percent in 2007. The growth declined sharply to 6.2 percent in 2008 and 6.6 percent in 2009. India has been much less export-dependent than China, and the export slowdown in India although sharp during the crisis, was much less intense than for China (Tables 1 and 2).

Table 2: Crisis and After: Select Economic Indicators of India

	2005	2006	2007	2008	2009	2010	2011
Gross domestic product, constant prices, % change	9.0	9.5	10.0	6.2	6.6	10.6	7.2
Total investment, % of GDP	34.2	35.3	37.3	34.6	37.1	35.4	34.4
Gross national savings, % of GDP	32.9	34.3	36.6	32.2	35.1	32.1	31.6
General government revenue, % of GDP	19.1	20.2	21.8	20.3	19.5	18.8	18.5
General government total expenditure, % of GDP	25.8	25.7	26.0	27.5	29.3	28.0	27.1
General government net lending/borrowing, % of GDP	−6.7	−5.5	−4.2	−7.2	−9.8	−9.2	−8.7
Inflation, average consumer prices, % change	4.0	6.3	6.4	8.3	10.9	12.0	8.6
Volume of imports of goods and services, % change	18.0	9.4	16.3	10.8	8.3	16.5	10.9
Volume of exports of goods and services, % change	18.9	13.8	17.1	10.6	0.8	21.9	14.5
Current account balance, % of GDP	−1.3	−1.0	−0.7	−2.5	−2.1	−3.3	−2.8

Source: International Monetary Fund, World Economic Outlook Database, April 2012.

An important characteristic of the Indian stimulus measures has been that they could not protect the savings and investment rates in the economy, which had been rising sharply before the crisis. On the contrary, both savings and investment rates declined sharply in the crisis year 2008, and could not reach the pre-crisis levels till as yet (Chart 2). India's savings had risen steadily from 32.9 of GDP in 2005 to 36.6 percent in 2007, but collapsed to 32.2 percent in 2008 and 35.1 percent in 2009. Investments had also increased from 34.2 percent of GDP in 2005 to 37.3 in 2007, but declined to 34.6 percent in 2008 and improved to 37.1 in 2009.

Chart 2: Savings and Investments in India, 2005–2011

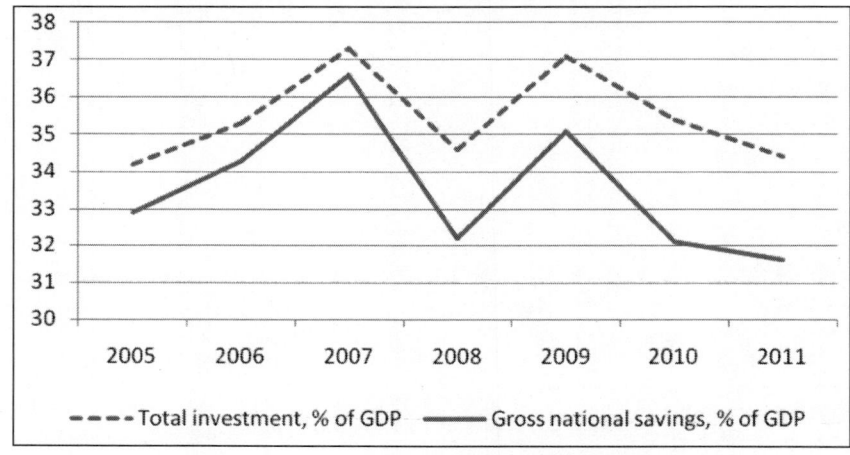

Source: IMF, World Economic Outlook Database, April 2012.

The government stimulus measures raised government expenditure from 26 percent of GDP in 2007 to 27.5 percent and 29.3 percent of GDP in 2008 and 2009 respectively. The fiscal deficit rose from 4.2 percent of GDP in 2007, to 7.2 percent in 2008 and to a larger 9.8 percent in 2009.

In fact, the policy measures implemented by the Indian government stimulated consumption and not investment. This is in marked contrast to the Chinese government measures which stimulated investment (Chart 3). The final consumption expenditure in India had been about 66 percent of GDP in 2007, and it went up sharply to 71 percent and 69 percent of GDP in 2008 and 2009 respectively. In China, on the other hand, consumption expenditure had been only 49.5 percent of GDP in 2007, which declined to about 48 percent in 2008, and 47 percent in 2009.

Chart 3: Consumption as percentage of GDP

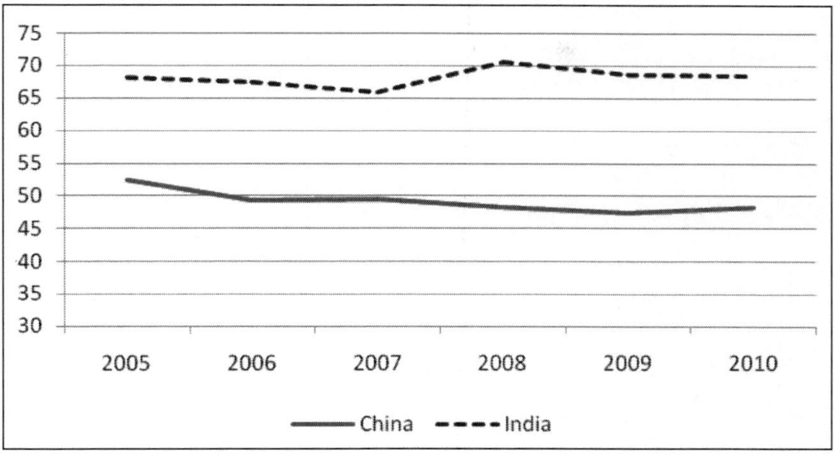

Source: World DataBank, World Bank, 2012.

Implications for the Future

As China's investment rates have risen, the crisis did not reduce the potential growth rate of the economy, and hence it would not be difficult to sustain a 10 percent + growth rate in the future for China. India, on the other hand, suffered a fall in its potential growth rate after the crisis, and that makes it really difficult for India to return to the pre-crisis rate of growth of 9–10 percent in the near future. This also accounts for the inability of India to reduce inflation for long, whereas China could very quickly bring inflation under control recently.

China undertook fiscal stimulus from a position of fiscal strength, and the rise in fiscal deficit during the crisis years has been within reasonable limits. Public debt in China had been below 20 percent of GDP at the end of 2007, and rose to about 34 percent of GDP, which is still low, at the end of 2010. India's large dose of fiscal stimulus have raised fiscal deficits high, and the public debt rose to over 73 percent of GDP at the end of 2008, but declined thereafter to 64 percent of GDP, a level considered still high, at the end of 2010.

While China retains a strong fiscal situation after the crisis, its financial sector has become weak with large amounts of bad loans. This resulted from bank-financing of a large part of the stimulus spending. On the other hand, India's financial sector was not much affected by the crisis, as the stimulus spending was mostly financed by the government budget, which has made the country's fiscal position rather weak after the crisis.

References

Joseph, Mathew (2009). 'Global Financial Crisis: How was India Impacted', Global Financial Governance—Challenges and Regional Responses, Conference Proceedings, September 3–4, Berlin, pp. 41–58.

Zhang, Liqing (2009). 'China's Policy Responses to the Global Financial Crisis: Efficacy and Risks', Global Financial Governance—Challenges and Regional Responses, Conference Proceedings, September 3–4, Berlin, pp. 59–64.

Does Chinese Renminbi Deserve Reserve Currency Status? A Challenging Road Ahead

Himanshu Joshi

FORE School of Management, New Delhi

E-mail: himanshu@fsm.ac.in

ABSTRACT

Against the backdrop of the global financial crisis, and more recent European debt crisis, the fate of two major currencies the US dollar and Euro as the premier international reserve currencies are under scrutiny. The 2010 central bank survey of foreign exchange market activity showed rapid growth in turnover in some emerging market currencies. China's growing stature in international trade, and its large net creditor's status make a strong case for the Chinese Renminbi becoming the premier international reserve currency, or at-least its inclusion in IMF's Special Drawing Rights (SDR). The article discusses the, benefits and costs of a currency getting the status of reserve currency, and explores the pre-requisites for the Chinese renminbi getting that status.

Keywords: Reserve Currency, US Dollar, Renminbi, Financial Crisis, Debt Crisis.

Introduction

Currency is an iconic expression of a country's economic dominance. The recent global financial crisis, and the more recent European debt crisis have forced international markets and economists to look for an alternative. Questions relating to reserve currency status become relevant and urgent under two conditions. First, when the policies of the principal reserve currency (US dollar) threaten to erode confidence in it, and second, when there is a possibility of ascendancy of another major currency from a large international trade economy having net creditor's status. Now the issue has resurfaced in the aftermath of the global financial crisis with somewhat greater intensity, because of a combination of two developments. First, there is a view that the crisis was occasioned in part by reckless US policies, that were in turn aided and abetted by the dollar's reserve currency role, which allowed the recklessness to be financed by outsiders (Subramanian 2011). The second reason relates to the rise of China as a major exporting country, and an economic growth engine for the global economy, with possible ascendancy of the Chinese renminbi to reserve currency status.

Table 1: China's Merchandise World Trade 1979–2010

(US $ billion)

Year	Exports	Imports	Trade Balance
1979	13.7	15.7	−2
1980	18.1	19.5	−1.4
1985	27.3	42.5	−15.2
1990	62.9	53.9	9
1995	148.8	132.1	16.7
2000	249.2	225.1	24.1
2001	266.2	243.6	22.6
2002	325.6	295.2	30.4
2003	438.4	412.8	25.6
2004	593.4	561.4	32
2005	762	660.1	101.9
2006	969.1	791.5	177.6
2007	1218	955.8	262.2
2008	1428.91	1131.5	297.41
2009	1202.01	1003.9	198.11
2010	1578.41	1393.9	184.51

Source: Global Trade Atlas.

Similar doubts about the dollar arose in the 1960s, which led to the creation of special drawing rights (SDRs), the international money created through the International Monetary Fund (IMF). The United States began to experience trade deficits with the rest of the world in the late 1950s, and the problem persisted into the 1960s. By the early 1960s, the total value of the US gold stock, when valued at US$ 35 per ounce, fell significantly short of foreign dollar holdings. This naturally created concern about the viability of the dollar-based system. To partially alleviate the pressure on the dollar as the central reserve currency, the IMF created an artificial international reserve called the SDR in 1970. The SDR, which is a basket currency, comprising major individual currencies, was allotted to members of the IMF, who could use it for transactions among themselves, or with the IMF. Now, in addition to gold and foreign exchanges, countries could use the SDR to make international payments.

Table 2: The Composition of the Special Drawing Right (SDR)

Currencies	1981–85	1986–90	1991–95	1996–2000	2001–2005	2006–2010
U.S. dollar	42%	42%	40%	39%	45%	41.9%
Euro	–	–	–	–	29	37.4
German mark	19	19	21	21	–	–
Japanese yen	13	15	17	18	15	9.4
British Pound	13	12	11	11	11	11.3
French franc	13	12	11	11	–	–

Source: Author's Reconstruction, The International Monetary Fund, data can be retrieved from http://www.imf.org/external/np/tre/sdr/sdrbasket.htm

Initially, the SDR was designed to be the weighted average of 16 currencies of those countries whose share in world exports were more than one percent. The percentage share of each currency in the SDR was about the same as the country's share in world exports. In 1981, however, the SDR was greatly simplified to comprise only five major currencies: The US dollar, German mark, Japanese yen, British pound and French franc. After the introduction of Euro as the common currency of the European Union in 2000, the German mark and French franc give way to Euro in SDR. The rising share of the Chinese exports in the global trade makes a strong case for inclusion of Chinese renminbi in SDR.

The article is further organized as follows. Section 2 discusses the costs and benefits to the country issuing reserve currency and explores the Chinese renminbi in that perspective, Section 3 analyzes the pre-requisite for any currency to get the reserve currency status and examines whether the Chinese renminbi deserves that status, Section 4 provides concluding remarks.

Benefits and Costs to the Country Issuing Reserve Currency

Benefits

Convenience for the Country's Residents: As per capita income of the country increases, its currency trades in greater multiples of the home economy's underlying international trade, and this is known as "financialisation of the currency." Country's exporters, importers, borrowers, and lenders are able to deal in their own currency, rather than foreign currencies. Thus, the transaction costs of obtaining another currency, and the psychological costs of having to move or convert from domestic to foreign currencies are lowered or eliminated.

Seigniorage or Exorbitant Privilege in Good Times: Seigniorage or Exorbitant Privilege is the ability to borrow abroad large amounts cheaply in one's own currency, especially while simultaneously earning much higher returns on investments including FDI in other countries. It can be interpreted as the ability to run large account deficits-and hence run up large debts denominated in one's own currency at lower interest rates-safe in the knowledge that others will be willing to finance it on account of the special status of the currency. The US has consistently earned more on its investments than it has had to pay on its debts, a differential of about 1.2 percent per annum (Cline 2005). A few recent studies indicate Seigniorage gains to US Bandholz, Clostermann, and Seitz (2009) found that the US treasury's 10 year bond yield was 70 basis point lower, as a result of foreign capital inflows. A recently released research report by Africa's largest bank Standard Group Bank, indicates increasing internationalization of the renminbi by 2015. It shows that 40 percent of the cino-African trade by 2015 will be denoted in Chinese renminbi. Since 2005, when China tweaked the Yuan-Dollar peg, it has risen by 28 percent, which works out to 4.5 percent per year. If you subtract out the two year period from 2008–2010 during which the Yuan was frozen in place, the appreciation has been closer to 7 percent per year, which makes it a preferred currency for investors.

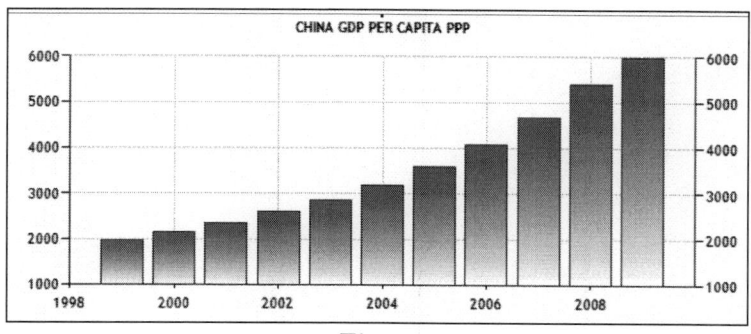

Fig. 1

Source: TradingEconomics.com, The World Bank Group.

Costs

Exorbitant or Seigniorage Curse: Seigniorage has a flip side. The fact that a currency is considered special makes it attractive to hold, increasing the demand for it, and causing the currency to appreciate and render exports less competitive on world markets. Bergsten (2009) indicates that the ability to finance current account deficits more easily, can lead to irresponsible government and private sector behaviour, thereby contributing to financial stability. The recent global financial crisis originating in US is a case in point. An exorbitant curve will also significantly affect the economic interests of China in global trades. As China is majorly an export oriented economy, higher demand for renminbi in international markets will cause its appreciation, and affect Chinese exports negatively.

Vulnerability from Exorbitant Privilege: Exorbitant privilege creates a vulnerability to external actions by investors in the currency. Volatility of the reserve currency increases substantially by the actions of external investors. When confidence of external investors in the reserve currency erodes, they offload their holdings in the market. China holds a large pile of US securities, and has some leverage over the US because of its ability to sell its large holdings of U.S. securities in the market, which may create instability complicating macro-economic management.

Prerequisites for a Reserve Currency Status

There are primarily three functions of a reserve currency: (1) store of value, which allows transactions to be conducted over long periods and geographical distances, (2) medium of exchange, and (3) unit of account, which facilitates valuation and calculation. Reserve currency is used equally by governments and private players in the international currency market. Governments use the reserve currency to store value of their foreign exchange reserves, to peg their local currency to the reserve currency, and as a vehicle for foreign exchange intervention to manage volatility of their domestic currencies. Private agents use the reserve currency as a means of payment in invoicing trade and financial transactions; they also use it as a store of value, and substitute for their domestic currencies, when the domestic currency is prone to inflation and volatility. Private agents also use the reserve currency as a swap currency for raising foreign capital at the lowest possible yield, and investing in foreign assets that provide the highest possible yields. Thus, the perquisite for any currency to provide store of value is, that there should be low and stable inflation in the country issuing the reserve currency, it should have a relatively strong and stable currency, should have deep and liquid financial markets open to foreign investors. Since 2005, when China tweaked the Yuan-Dollar pegs, it has risen by 28 percent, which works out to 4.5 percent per year. If you subtract out the two year period from 2008–2010 during which the Yuan was frozen in place, the appreciation has been closer to 7 percent per year, that makes it a preferred currency for investors. As far as China's inflation is concerned, it has been quite volatile, still China is giving the highest positive GDP growth figures in the world, which makes the Chinese renminbi a hard currency. For a currency to function as a medium of exchange for government and private agents, the issuing country must have a large global share of output, trade and finance. China's growing role in world trade makes a strong case for the renminbi to get the status of a reserve currency. However, existence of deep, liquid and open financial markets is also a crucial prerequisite for the currency to be used as a medium of exchange; renminbi does not sail through comfortably against US dollar, or even the Euro on this criterion.

The 2010 central bank survey of the foreign exchange market activity showed rapid growth in turnover in the emerging markets. In particular, global central banks reported that some up-and-coming currencies traded outside their home market to a much greater extent, than the expectations of the market participants. Chinese renminbi's offshore trading was recorded as US$ 22 billion against expectations of US$ 3 billion. Similarly, offshore trading of the Indian rupee was recorded at US$ 17 billion much higher than

China Inflation Rate
Annual Change on Consumer Price Index

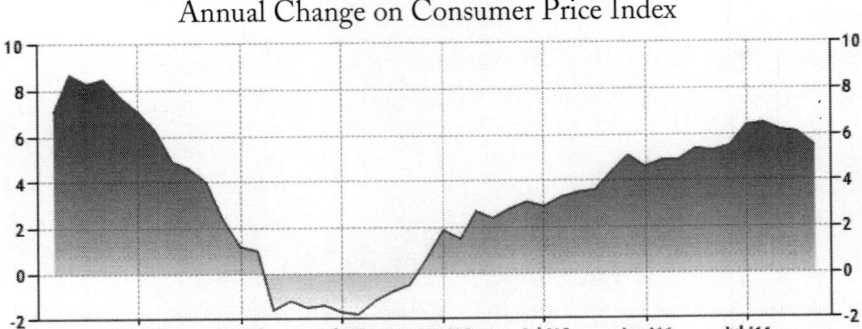

India Inflation Rate
Annual Change on Consumer Price Index

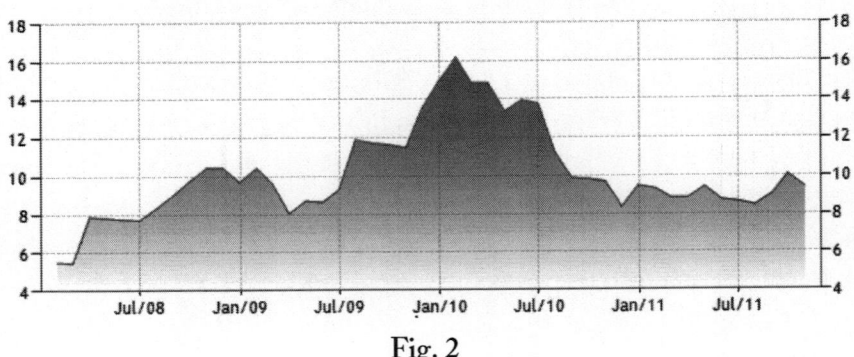

Fig. 2

Source: tradingeconomics.com

expected by the market participants. Global turnover figures for the Chinese renminbi and the Indian rupee were quite close, at the respective US$ 34 billion and US$ 38 billion, which is quite surprising as the Chinese economy is both larger and more open than that of India, so the similar absolute dollar figures translate into ratios that differ by an order of magnitude. Thus, we can intuitively say that the renminbi trades less than China's trade and income would suggest, while the rupee trades more than India's trade and income would seem to warrant. Part of the difference may arise from the high portfolio investments in the Indian equity market open for foreign investors, in contrast to the closed Chinese equity market. A second factor that is increasingly influencing a cross section of the global turnover is the level of yields: higher-yielding and lower-yielding currencies turn over more. International private agents borrow in low-yielding currencies to fund investments in high yielding currency securities. Chinese government securities are not open for foreign investors, and raising money in closed Chinese financial markets is a difficult task for international private agents. Thus, the renminbi neither serves as a financing currency nor as investment currency. McCauley and Scatigna (2011) show that as the country income per capital rises, a currency trades in ever greater multiples of the home economy's underlying international trade (financialisation) and trades to greater extent outside its home market (internationalization). They used Income per capita as proxy for a number of related aspects, such as financial depth and complexity, creditworthiness. It also serves a proxy for store of value. They used the ratio of foreign exchange turnover in a given currency to its issuing country's summation of exports and imports, and called it foreign exchange turnover to trade ratio. They plot this ratio against the GDP per capita of the respective economies. Their analysis shows that renminbi trades in daily amounts are similar to daily Chinese exports and imports of goods and services-a ratio of around 1. Other currencies, such as the US dollar or Japanese yen, trade in amounts closer to 100 times the value of corresponding international trade transactions. The reason for this dispersion is explained by the fact that as economies develop; trading of their currencies grows faster than their current account transactions. Currencies also show a wide dispersion in the geography of trading. Some currencies trade largely in their home market, either between two residents (strictly domestic trading), or between one resident and a non-resident (onshore-offshore trading). Others trade for the most part outside the home market between two non residents (strictly off-shore trading). Currencies of higher income countries tend to trade more outside the home jurisdiction, which is an important prerequisite for any currency to become the reserve currency. The result of their analysis shows that among the three major currencies, the Euro has the highest ratio of offshore transactions, especially in London, than do the US dollar and Japanese yen. The currencies of many low—to medium income countries trade offshore to a greater or lesser extent than the norm. Off-shore trading of the Indian rupee lines up with India's income. Strictly off-shore trading bulks large for the Chinese renminbi in a non-deliverable form. The high share of off-shore trading, the dearth of on-shore off-shore trading, and rapid development of the deliverable renminbi market in Hong Kong SAR reflect the gap between the world's interest in the renminbi and its access to it.

Concluding Remark

China's growing role in global trade, low to moderate and stable Inflation, strong and continuously appreciating currency against the existing SDR currency portfolio, high ratio of offshore trading makes a strong case for the renminbi to get the status of an official reserve currency. However, a very low ratio of its foreign exchange turnover to trade (1:1) in comparison to the same for the US dollar and Japanese yen (over 100:1), its controlled equity market and low depth financial market pose challenges to becoming a reserve currency. If, relative to China's trade and income, the renminbi turnover were to reach Indian rupee like levels, the case for its inclusion in the SDR would be strengthened. Renminbi's inclusion in SDR will also reduce later's volatility, as almost all the SDR currencies in the recent past are depreciating against the renminbi.

References

Bank of International Settlements (2010a). *80th Annual Report*, June.

Bank of International Settlements (2010b). *Triennial Central Bank Survey: Report on global foreign exchange market activity in 2010*, December.

Ho, C., Ma, G. and McCauley, R. (2005). "Trading Asian currencies", *BIS Quarterly Review*, March, pp. 49–58.

HSBC (2009). *HSBC's emerging markets currency guide 2010*, December.

International Monetary Fund (2010). *Review of the method of valuation of the SDR*, 26 October.

McCauley, R. (2010). "Internationalizing the Australian dollar", in C. Shu and W. Peng (eds.), *Currency Internationalization: International experiences and implications for the renminbi*, Palgrave Macmillan, Basingstoke.

Subramanian, A., "Renminbi Rules: The Conditional Imminence of the Reserve Currency Transition", *Peterson Institute for International Economics Working Paper WP 11–14*, September 2011.

Tsuyuguchi, Y. and Wooldridge, P. (2008). "The evolution of trading activity in Asian foreign exchange market", *BIS Working Papers*, No. 252, May.

The Hukou System in China: An Overview

Neeraj Kumar

FORE School of Management, New Delhi

E-mail: neeraj@fsm.ac.in

ABSTRACT

In 1958, the "Regulations on Household Registration in the People's Republic of China," popularly known as the Hukou System was passed in China. This system traditionally served three main purposes: Resource distribution, migration control and monitoring of a targeted group of people. The Hukou was used to erect a largely hereditary system that divided China's agricultural and non-agricultural populations, and effectively bound the peasantry to the land they tilled. Over the years, however, while implementation of this system has unintentionally created a vast pool of cheap labour for industrialization of China, it has also, in its wake, generated inequalities in the social and regional development, leading to social tension.

Keywords: Migrant Labour, Urbanisation, Household-Registration, Social-Security.

Introduction

On coming to power in China in 1949, the Chinese Communist Party (CCP) patterned its' economic development on the lines of the Soviet model, hoping to fuel urban industrialization through surpluses in agriculture. To create a surplus in agriculture, it was important to collectivise farms and to ensure that farmers stayed rooted to the farm to boost agricultural production. To doubly ensure that the rural peasantry contributed their labour to agriculture alone, the CCP abolished all non-agriculture sources of income for the peasants through traditional means such as handicrafts, entrepreneurship, local trading, animal husbandry etc. Towards this end, a series of initiatives were taken, one of which was the Hukou and the consequent legal segregation of urban and rural Chinese, and also agricultural and non-agricultural China.

Soon after the CCP's coming to power in 1949, state policy also sought to foster a balanced regional development of the regions, specially industrial development between the coastal region and non-coastal inland. From 1952 to 1957, therefore, non-coastal provinces received substantial investments from the state for industrial development. New industries came up in cities across the whole of China, and not just in the coastal areas. These were State Owned Enterprises (SOEs). Growth of cities attracted people from the devastated countryside, the prosperity of developing cities giving hope for livelihoods. This appeared to be the only option for an economically better life by the rural multitudes. The first wave of migration, therefore, started from the rural areas towards the urban centres. Massive migration took place between 1949 and 1957.

Alarmed by mind-boggling migration and fearing social unrest, the Chinese political apparatus started issuing directives to slow down rural migration to cities from 1953 onwards. Detention centres were established at various places, to detain and return the peasants to their places of origin. But these measures were not enough. In 1958, the National People's Congress passed its "Regulations on Household Registration in the People's Republic of China", popularly known as the Hukou system.

The Objectives of the Hukou System

*The stated objective of Hukou System wa*s "to maintain social order, protect citizens' rights and benefits, and to serve in the construction of socialism."[1] The Hukou system traditionally served three main purposes: Resource distribution, migration control and monitoring of targetted groups of people.[2] Its most significant effect, however, was to employ the *hukou* to erect a largely hereditary system that divided China's agricultural and non-agricultural populations, and effectively bound the peasantry to the land they tilled.[3]

The Hukou Dual Classification

Hukou is one of the most important mechanisms determining entitlement to public welfare and urban services. To understand the 'system,' it is important to know that the mainland Chinese' 'hukou' is categorized in two ways: a) by socio-economic eligibility and, b) by residential location.

Socio-Economic Eligibility

The first classification of Hukou registration is the Hukou "type" or "nature," commonly referred to as "agricultural" and "non-agricultural" Hukou. In the pre liberalized years (1958 to the late 70s), this classification determined entitlement to state-subsidized food grain (called "commodity grain") and other prerogatives. An approximate equivalent would be the ration cards issued to urban dwellers in India, though there are significant differences. The difference between agricultural and nonagricultural status is (was) the main determinant of eligibility to receive a variety of state-provided socio-economic benefits (till the eighties). The non-agricultural Hukou status entitled a Chinese citizen to state-provided social benefits, and security (eg house, employment, subsidized grains, education, health service etc). The population with agricultural type Hukou categorisation was expected to be largely self-sufficient, receiving very limited, if any, state largesse. Those with non-agricultural status, regardless of their physical location, or whether they resided in a town, small city or large city, were automatically entitled to these benefits, because they were distributed and funded by the central government, making non-agricultural status highly desired throughout the country. Those with agricultural status had no legal means by which to obtain these resources, either inside or outside their registered location. This mechanism served to curb migration outside the state plan. Moreover, transferring status from agricultural to non-agricultural was subject to strict regulation and control by the central government.[4]

Residential Location: Local and Non-Local Hukou

In addition to the Hukou "type," all individuals are also categorized according to their *place* of Hukou registration. This is one's official or "permanent" residence. Under Hukou regulations, each citizen is required to register in one and only one place of permanent residence. In other words, in addition to the agricultural and non-agricultural classification, everyone is also distinguished by whether or not they have a local Hukou with respect to an administrative unit (such as a city, town or village). The local regular Hukou registration defines one's rights for many activities in a specific locality. The Hukou 'type' defined the type of services and welfare available to individuals (usually stipulated by the central government), and the Hukou 'place' determined where individuals would receive them.[5,6] These changes have resulted in increasingly greater variations among different urban jurisdictions in the amount and types of services and privileges available to local Hukou holders. Since the two classifications of Hukou (type and location) mean different things, cities and towns have both non-agricultural and agricultural Hukou population living in them and, conversely, agricultural Hukou population may exist in the countryside, and in the cities. Therefore, until recently, in any city there were four types of people, excluding foreign nationals, based on the dual classifications of Hukou. For example, if we consider Beijing, then it would have four categories as follows:

1. Those holding local (Beijing) and non-agricultural Hukou (including most Beijing "urban residents," as they are commonly known).
2. Those holding local and agricultural Hukou (most of whom live in Beijing's outlying districts and counties).
3. Those holding non-local (non-Beijing) and non-agricultural Hukou (mostly migrants from other cities), and
4. Those holding non-local and agricultural Hukou (mostly migrants from the countryside outside Beijing; a great majority of the rural, peasant migrants are in this category).

Migrant Labour

It is the fourth category which is a matter of concern, both within and outside China, largely because this is a group that is largely deprived of any public service, social benefits or other beneficience of the state. It is this category that is referred to as migrant labour, or the floating population of China. Many scholars have argued that exploitation of this cheapest form of labour has given a competitive advantage to the Chinese manufactured goods. '…a key reason why Chinese economic development—especially its export led growth—has been so impressive, is because of its peculiar Hukou system, a powerful institution of organizing and managing people that is the most important and plentiful resource that China has.'[7] The number of the fourth category has increased manifold in China during the past two decades. This has happened due to several reasons some of which are:

- Privatization of agriculture, rendering labour surplus in the countryside.
- Wide scale industrialization due to the opening up of the economy, and consequently an increased demand for labour in the industrializing urban centres.

- Loosening of controls in the administration of the Hukou system, devolving of powers to administer the system at the local level, to the provincial or the local governments.

These changes unleashed large waves of migration. The total number of migrant labour in China is estimated to range between 140 million to 210 million people. Arguably, it is the low cost of employing this labour that has provided an advantage to the export led economy of China. The status of this labour is akin to illegal migrant labour in the EU or the USA, or even India. However, this labour in China has two important differences—they are illegals in their own country, and the total number of this labour as a proportion of total labour in China is very large. Because of their uncertain status, this group has no legal or social protection and is exploited by employers. The success of China as an economic power has not been without costs. While the Hukou system has created a vast pool of cheap labour, it has also generated inequalities in the social and regional development, leading to social tensions.

Bibliography

Kam Wing Chan, 'Urban Myth', South China Post, August 24, 2011.

Report of Congressional-Executive Commission On China, 'China's Household Registration System: Sustained Reform Needed to Protect China's Rural Migrants', 7th Oct, 2005, accessed at www.cecc.gov on 5th Dec., 2011.

Tiejun Cheng; Mark Selden, The Origins and Social Consequences of China's Hukou System, *The China Quarterly*, No. 139. (Sep., 1994) accessed at http://links.jstor.org/sici?sici=0305-7410%28199409% 290%3A139%3C644%3ATOASCO%3E2.0.CO%3B2-1

Li Shi, Rural Migrant Workers in China: Scenario, Challenges and Public Policy, Working Paper No. 89 (June 2008), Policy Integration and Statistics Department, International Labour Office, Geneva.

Binggin Li and David Piachaud, Urbanization and Social Policy in China, Asia-Pacific Development Journal, Vol. 13, No. 1, June 2006.

References

LexisNexis, http://hk.lexiscn.com/law/regulations-of-the-peoples-republic- of-china-on-household-registration.html?eng=0, accessed on 9ᵗʰ Dec, 2011.

"China's Household Registration System: Sustained Reform Needed to Protect China's Rural Migrants", Congressional—Executive Commission on China (CECC) Report accessed on 9ᵗʰ Dec, 2011 at http://www.ecc.gov/pages/news/hukou.php

Hayden Windrow, Anik Guha The Hukou System, Migrant Workers and State Power in the People's Republic of China, Northwestern University Journal of International Human Rights, Volume 3 (JULY 2005), Accessed On 8ᵗʰ December 2011 AT 3 Nw. U. J. Int'l Hum. Rts. 3 *at* http://www.law.northwestern.edu/journals/jihr/v3/3.

Chan and Buckingham, 'Is China Abolishing the Hukou System?', The China Quarterly, 2008 doi:10.1017/S030574100800078 accessed at http://faculty.washington.edu/stevehar/Chan%20and%20Buckingham.pdf on 7ᵗʰ Dec 2011

Chan and Buckingham, 'Is China Abolishing the Hukou System?', The China Quarterly, 2008 doi:10.1017/S030574100800078 accessed at http://faculty.washington.edu/stevehar/Chan%20and%20Buckingham.pdf on 7ᵗʰ Dec 2011.

Wang, Fei Ling, 'A Success Tough to Duplicate: The Chinese Hukou System', 'Fair Observer' accessed at ttp://fairobserver.com/article/ success-tough-duplicate-chinese-hukou-system?

Wang, Fei Ling, 'A Success Tough to Duplicate: The Chinese Hukou System', 'Fair Observer' accessed at ttp://fairobserver.com/article/ success-tough-duplicate-chinese-hukou-system?

The Chinese Economy: Economic Objectives and Growth Indicators

Kanhaiya Singh

FORE School of Management, New Delhi
E-mail: kanhaiya@fsm.ac.in

ABSTRACT

There are many myths about the Chinese economic growth, . economic life and its future growth prospects. The rapid economic growth of China, more so, in the last two decades surpassed many other developed and developing economies. The picture represented by the Chinese government on various developmental issues looks quite rosy. But, then experts the world over have their conflicting views over the speed of growth. We often come across that the data presented by the Chinese government cannot be taken at face value. Some of the experts and economists from other countries have made considerable research to verify the statistics provided by the China government. They have gone to study economic life in the rural areas of China. The findings of these research studies are surprising and do not subscribe to the growth history per-se of China. In this article an attempt is made to compile the available information on various economic issues and patterns and the opinion of experts from different countries including international monetary organizations.

Keywords: GDP, Per Capita Income, Savings Growth, Foreign Exchange Reserves, Socio-Economic Conditions.

Introduction

GDP growth in China was 10.3 percent in 2010. GDP for China in 2010 was US$ 5.88 trillion ahead of Japan's US$ 5.45 trillion.

GDP in China was US$ 4.91 trillion in 2009, compared to US$ 14 trillion in the United States. GDP in China rose from US$ 1.3 trillion in 2001 to US$ 3.6 trillion in 2008. Per capita GDP in China is one seventh that of the United States. It will take considerable time for China to catch up with the United States in terms of wealth. According to the China government estimates the per capita income in China in 2050 will still be about half that of the United States. Per capita income in China in 2008 was US$ 2,369, which ranked 132nd internationally, ahead of Cape Verde and behind Guatemala. Per capita income in the United States is US$ 46,040.

China is the fastest growing major economy. It has been that way for more than a decade, and is expected to remain that way for the next 5 to 10 years. In the mid 2000s, China passed France, Italy and Britain to become the world's fourth largest economy and passed Germany as the world third largest economy in 2007. China's GNP quintupled between 1990 and 2001 when it reached US$ 1.3 trillion, smaller than the US$ 4.3 trillion GDP of Japan but larger than the US$ 737 billion in the 10 Southeast Asian members of ASEAN. Economic output reached US$ 2.3 trillion in 2005 and US$ 2.7 trillion in 2006 (US$ 2.054 per person), compared to US$ 13.2 trillion in 2006 (US$ 43,950 per person) in the United States. Even within China, the GDP in different regions varies to a higher degree as per capita GDP in Beijing reached US$ 10,000 in 2009 for the first time. In 2008, output per person in China was US$ 2,500. A poll conducted by the Pew Research Center before the 2008 Olympics found that 82 percent of the Chinese interviewed were satisfied with national economy growth. They indicated that the growth was up from 52 percent in 2002. The International Monetary Fund's Economic Outlook Database, ranked China 109th between Swaziland and Morocco (2008). In the international competitiveness ranking in 2007, China ranked 15th. The United States ranked 1st; Singapore was 2nd; Japan was 24th.

China Surpasses Japan as the World's Second Largest Economy

In the April–June quarter of 2010, China surpassed Japan as the world's second largest economy, as it chalked up US$ 1.337 trillion of GDP in that period compared to US$ 1.288 trillion for Japan according to Japanese government statistics. Japan's per capita income is still 10 times higher than that of China, and the Chinese government still has great challenges ahead of it and many obstacles such as population, income disparities and unhappy have-nots to overcome. In terms of GDP, China overtook Britain and France in 2005 and Germany in 2007. In 2009, China surpassed Germany to become the world's largest exporter. Explaining his interpretation of how Japan became number three William Pesek of Bloomberg wrote: 'In China you have 1.3 billion people working hard to circumvent government regulations to make a quick Yuan. Japan has 126 million complaining about how the government isn't fixing their lives." In 2007 China surpassed Germany to become the world third largest economy. Goldman Sachs predicts that China will surpass the United States and become the world's largest economy in 2027 and will be twice as large as the American economy in 2050 as domestic demand really begins to kick in. Price Waterhouse Cooper has predicted that China could surpass the United States as early as 2020. The Carnegie Endowment for International Peace predicted that it would occur by 2035. Goldman Sachs economist Jim O'Neil has predicted that China will eclipse the United States as the world's No.1 economy in 2027.

Characteristics of the Chinese Economy

China has managed to combine Communist ideology and free-for-all capitalism in its rawest form, to create what the government calls a "socialist market" through using Chinese traditions to justify its authoritarian hold of the government and control of free market forces. China is essentially a developing country with some characteristics of a developed economy and is simultaneously experiencing industrial and information age revolutions. While the majority of the population toils on peasant farmsteads, information age research centers are opening up and factories are producing advanced electronics. Many economists feel that anything less than 8 percent growth is like a recession in China, because of the need to create jobs and support the growing labour market.

Eight percent growth is regarded as the minimum for maintaining social stability. Yale's Stephen Roach wrote in the *Christian Science Monitor*, "Services account for just 43 percent of Chinese GDP—well below global norms. Services are an important piece of China's pro-consumption strategy—especially large-scale transactions-based industries such as distribution (wholesale and retail), domestic transportation, supply-chain logistics, and hospitality and leisure. Over the next five years, the services share of Chinese GDP could rise above the currently targeted four-percentage-point increase. This is a labour-intensive, resource-efficient, environmentally-friendly growth recipe—precisely what China needs in the next phase of its development. Japanese Sinolgist Mineo Nakajama told *Time*, "China is like a movie set. It looks wonderful, but it's all illusion." Under the surface there are problems like real estate bubble, industrial over capacity, rampant corruption, debt-ridden banks and companies.

Objectives of Chinese Economic Growth

China adopted the reforms path through institutional innovation, following the model of regional development. The farmers in rural areas were given residual ownership, wherein they could retain certain returns on pre fixed parameters. This motivated people at large and resulted in increased output and household savings. The urban segment too was promoted by allowing them to retain a certain portion of their profits, introducing reforms in the wage system, employment guarantee and social security system. On the industrial growth front, China adopted many policy measures such as development of special economic zones, free trade zones, high technology development zones. This model, export led growth of China helped it to increase its exports to GDP ratio from 15 percent in 1990 to 30 percent in 2000.

It can be said that China's experiments to promote regional growth and steps towards moving from a planned economy to market driven economy to an extent paved the way for the success of the private sector and decelerated role of the public sector. Though in the initial stages, there was not much clarity and objectivity in the minds of policy makers, but the extent of success changed sentiments and there was a great shift towards a market oriented economy. However, there remains certain issues which need consideration for future development prospects:

(a) There seems to be a strong relationship between state, state owned enterprises and state owned banks. The government has leverage to effect the financing decisions the corporates and thereby the efficiency and performance of these enterprises. In the urban segment, the state sector is decentralized to a great extent, but inefficiencies in resources allocation may bring imbalances in realizing comprehensive advantages.

(b) The growth model of China per-se, has a major focus on urban development, but nearly 60 percent of its population is dependent on agriculture. Many persons have migrated from the rural areas to urban places. This will again cause imbalances in rural and urban development.

(c) A well defined formal property rights are lacking. It is only in Beijing where protection equals public property to private property are defined and granted protection. Though there has been economic growth, but for sustainable growth the structural issues need to be addressed.

Macroeconomic View

The currency of China is called the Yuan, Renminbi (RMB), or kuai. One Yuan is divided into 10 jiao or mao (fen, or cents are no longer used). Tiananmen Square is pictured on every note of the Chinese currency. Mao Zedong is pictured on 100 Yuan banknotes. Sun Yat-sen is on others. In the old days, the Yuan used by ordinary Chinese had images of factories and happy rural workers, while those used by foreign tourists looked like "cigarette coupons from the 1950s" and had images of scenic areas on one side and instructions on how to use them on the other. In April, 2008 the Yuan rose past seven to the dollar for the first time since the fixed exchange rate ended in 2006. It broke the 7.5 to the dollar mark in October 2007. The Yuan rose around 9 percent in 2007 and 4.4 percent in the first three months of 2008. The exchange rate for the Yuan was 7.97 in 2006, 8.19 in 2005, 8.27 in 2002, 2003 and 2004.

Economic Statistics of China

The Gross Domestic Product (GDP) of China was US$ 4.91 trillion in 2009. Composition by sector: agriculture 11.7 percent; industry, including construction: 48.9 percent; services: 39.8 percent. Per capita income (GNP per person): US$ 2,369 to US$ 3,300 in 2008. Estimates vary widely. In 2007 the World Bank estimated per capita GDP to be US$ 7,000 but planned to lower this estimate by 40 percent. The CIA Fact book lists a figure of US$ 1,740 for 2007. In any case, China has managed to double its per capita outcome in 10 years, compared to 34 years in Japan.

The unemployment rate in China was 4.9 percent in February 2010 and 4.2 percent in urban areas in 2005. These figures are of dubious validity. There is a lot of unemployment and underemployment in rural areas.

Savings rate: 49.7 percent of GDP, the highest in the world.

Some of the statistics that have been released by Beijing are highly suspect and unreliable. Foreign companies that do business in China don't trust Chinese statistics, especially at the local level, and do their own basic research before investing. China has a long tradition of quota fudging. Growth figures are sometimes wildly inflated, because output of small- and medium-sized companies is grossly overestimated. Even so, some economists believe that true growth figures are actually a couple of percentage points below the ones that are listed. Some have wondered if the results from the 2010 census are accurate. A common concern among Chinese (and non Chinese) is that official figures are fudged to create a false sense of optimism.

Guo Ying, a 31-year-old office worker in Beijing, said "The final result might not be true and therefore it would be meaningless. Some figures are said to be found through investigation, but is that true? A lot of people have their doubts. Figures like the CPI (consumer price index), the GDP, do they reflect the real situation? Many people are skeptical." John Lee wrote in *Newsweek*, "It is hard to judge China's state-led economy. The government's actions lie hidden beneath hundreds of tons of secrecy, and beyond easy measurement. China's quarterly growth statistics are often "policy-engineered" and after they are released, China analysts immediately begin second-guessing them. An analyst asked how are the figures arrived at, and he said, "Every quarter, the National Bureau of Statistics goes through the same ritual. Statistics come in from all over the country.

The provinces compile them with impossible speed—around two weeks, or three times as fast as many developed economies with much more efficient processes of data collection.[*Source:* John Lee, *Newsweek*, July 30, 2010, Lee is a foreign-policy research fellow at the Center for Independent Studies and a visiting fellow at the Hudson Institute in Washington, D.C. He is the author of *Will China Fail?* The NBS sorts through them, "consults" with senior CCP officials, applies a mysterious methodology to trim them into shape, and then spits out a figure that is uncannily well aligned with the targets set by political masters in Beijing. After several years, provincial historical data is tediously retrieved and analyzed by Chinese economists, and official figures are revised. Significant discrepancies are discovered and condemned, ending with Beijing promising to meticulously address the "structural flaws" in the statistical gathering process.

The official numbers are derived from reporting by local officials. These officials have massive incentives to tell Beijing what it wants to hear as regards hitting central targets—whether it be breakneck growth, or an engineered slowdown. It is the basis for their promotion. While the upside for dishonesty is obvious, there is usually little downside, as it's unlikely they will be caught, let alone punished, for fudging figures. Dodgy accounting practices, according to John Makin, in a piece for the American Enterprise think tank, include counting goods as sold when they leave factories, not when they are actually bought by consumers, and counting bank loans towards GDP as soon as they are disbursed, even if companies hoard the cash, or use the money to buy shares. Dodgy statistics is not in itself the most serious problem.

In China's state-dominated approach, the incapacity to effectively govern such a vast country is the real and pressing issue. The common Western view of "market socialism" as a ruthlessly efficient system, when it comes to top-down policy implementation, ignores the reality that proper verification of any official number is almost impossible. Seeking truth from facts is a wise and pragmatic piece of advice for reforming China. But getting the facts first could be the hard part. To beef up statistics, government accountants add income from single collectively-owned pig to five villagers, instead of just one; and cadres borrow goats from neighbouring villages so their villages look more affluent than they really are when inspectors come. Looking after a cow for a day gives a person a right to claim that as an asset. Selling any amount of produce is recorded as profit. In some cases, these statistics make villages where people are hungry and poor, seem like bustling income earners.

Sometimes economic data and statistics are made up to suit propaganda needs, a tradition that dates back to the Mao era, when making the party happy was the primary concern. In many cases, accountants are under specific orders to create rosy scenarios and statistics reflect government-ordered targets and quotas not reality. Local officials inflate and go along with the schemes, because they worry they will be demoted if they don't.

Economic Power Growth in China

The growth of China has averaged over 10 percent in the last 30 years. It was 9.4 percent between 1978 and 1995. It was 11.2 percent between 1990 and 1998 and 11.2 percent between 1990 and 1998 and just under 10 percent between 1999 and 2007. Growth rate: 11.4 percent in 2007; 11.1 percent in 2006; 10.2 percent in 2005, 10.1 percent in 2004; 9.1 percent in 2003; 6.7 on 1999; 7.8 in 1998; 8.8 percent in 1997; 9.6 in 1996; 10.5 percent in 1995; 12.6 percent in 1994; 13.5 percent in 1993; 14.2 percent in 1992; 9.2 percent in 1991; 3.8 percent in 1990. Growth was 10.3 percent in 2010. Growth of 9.7 percent in the first quarter of 2011 and 9.5 percent in the second quarter of 2011. Many economists feel that anything less than 8 percent growth is like a recession in China, because of the need to create jobs and support the growing labour market. Eight percent growth is regarded as the minimum for maintaining social stability. Economists also say that China could grow at the rate of 8 to 10 percent for some years, by simply adopting known technologies and ending obvious inefficiencies.

Suspect Growth Statistics for China

Lewis Thurow an economist at MIT is very skeptical about China's growth figures. He argues that if anything, they reflect the growth rate in the cities but not the countryside where two thirds of China's population lives. Even government figures indicate that growth in China's rural areas is minimal. If the double digits growth rates were true then China's cities wold have to have a 33 percent growth rate. Thurow also points to electricity consumption as an indicator of China's suspect statistics. Growth rates can be ascertained by electric consumption rates, because almost all forms of production require electricity. Because of inefficiencies electric consumption rates always exceed growth rates. But, that is not true in China, where many provinces post economic growth rates that are higher than electricity consumption. Based on statistics of electricity consumption rates and rural growth Thurow concluded that growth rates in China are between 5 and 6 percent, not 10 and 11 percent. The 10 percent to 11 percent is the growth rate in the cities.

Economics and Life in China

Richard Komaiko wrote in the *Asia Times*, "Westerners often focus myopically on the growth rate of China's gross domestic product (GDP), which is roughly 9 percent per year. While this is an important indicator of prosperity, it must be considered in tandem with other important metrics, such as inflation and the increasing cost of residential real estate. China's consumer price index rose 5 percent in the first quarter of 2011. This means that the effective real growth rate in GDP was only 4 percent. On top of that, the cost of real estate in many cities is growing at 20 percent per year. Considering these numbers, put yourself in the shoes of the average recent college graduate in a city like Shanghai. [*Source:* Richard Komaiko, Asia Times May 25, 2011.

"You make a decent income, but you can't afford to make a down payment on a piece of real estate, so you rent for a few years. But because the price of real estate is growing many times faster as the overall economy, the longer you wait, the less you can afford to buy. And in Chinese culture, if you can't afford a home, you can't start a family, and so forth."

Inflation in China

China has traditionally been very cheap. In the 1980s, one could pay 16 cents to be admitted into a public bath which provided a piece of soap, a towel and a bed. After the Deng economic reforms began taking hold in the 1980s, it began increasing. Consumer inflation rose 17.5 percent in 1989; 3 percent 1991; 5 percent 1992; 13 percent 1993; 27 percent in 1994. The price of many basic foods and grains increased 60 percent in the early 1990s. Inflation was running at 5 percent and 6 percent in the 2000s, with prices for things like textiles, cell phones and cars falling, while those for gasoline and food rose. The government has used price controls to keep inflation in check. In 2005, as some inflation pressures were easing, there was discussion of lifting price controls. In recent years, high inflation has been painful for the average Chinese. Soaring prices for pork, vegetables and other staples have authorities worried about the potential for social unrest. So has a property bubble that has put home ownership out of reach of millions, exacerbating the gulf between the rich and poor. The poor suffer the most. Poor families spend up to half their incomes on food and are hard hit by high price rises. Businesses, meanwhile, have to cope with rising labour costs, energy shortages and higher borrowing costs. The Chinese government is fearful of high inflation. Through China's history, major social upheavals and unrest have occurred when prices were high and people took to the streets to protest. High prices was one of the main forces behind the Tiananmen Square protests in 1989.

High inflation endangers China's status as a low-cost workshop for the world. It also limits China's ability to offset slowdowns by launching new stimulus packages. If the government's efforts to fight inflation cause the economy to stumble, that will cloud the outlook for international businesses—whether multinationals like General Electric or copper miners in Chile—that have been counting on China for growth. Food prices account for a third of the consumer price index used to measure inflation. "Actual numbers are worse than officially reported," Carmen M. Reinhart, an economist at the Peterson Institute for International Economics in Washington, told the *New York Times*. Chinese and Western economists say that the index understates the true extent of inflation because of methodology problems. The National Bureau of Statistics has said that it is trying to improve the index.

High Inflation in China in 2010 and 2011

Inflation in China rose 5.1 percent in November 2010, the first time it exceeded 5 percent in two years. This was on the heels of a 4.4 percent rise in October, followed by a 4.6 percent rise in December. The government anticipated price increases and took measures to boost supplies of goods whose supplies were reduced by summer floods and winter cold napes, but the measures did not work and prices were higher than had been anticipated. Consumer price inflation was 5.4 percent in the first three months of 2011. Many experts believe that the true figure is higher. In January, food prices rose 10.3 percent, with a 34.8 percent rise increase in fresh fruit prices and a 20.2 percent rise in the price of eggs. Inflation remained relatively high despite a series of government measures including three recent interest-rate increases. "Inflation is like a tiger; once it gets free, it is difficult to put it back in the cage," Premier Wen said. Consumer price inflation eased slightly to 5.3 percent in April on the back of a 11.5 percent in food cost, and was well above the government target of 4 percent.

Inflation reached a 34 month high of 5.5 percent in May 2011 driven by 11.7 percent food costs, which had increased due to demand exceeding supply, and the affects of drought, floods and other weather-related problems on crops. McDonald's raised the prices of its hamburgers and drinks by 10 percent. Inflation was up 6.4 percent, with food prices up 14.4 percent, in June 2011, rising further to 6.5 percent (a 37 month high), with food prices up 14.8 percent, in July, then dropped to 6.2 percent, with food prices up 14.8 percent, in August. Crop damage attributed to heavy rains and summer floods contributed to the high prices. Analysts have said that current price hikes are much more serious than those seen in previous years, with the cost of everything from land to labour to raw materials all climbing. "Inflation pressures are far more stubborn this time because the structural inflation is a much bigger problem than it was at any time in the last decade," Ben Simpfendorfer, according to Managing Director of economic consultancy firm China Insider.

GDP Per Capita in China—Conflicting Data

The GDP per head numbers vary according to the source. According to the IMF, China has a per capita income in 2009 of US$ 6,546, just above Ukraine and just below Namibia. According to the World Bank it had a GDP per capita of US$ 3,700 just ahead of Albania but behind more than 100 other countries. According to the 2010 Chinese census, per capita GDP reached a respectable US$ 4,300. Per capita annual income estimates in 2011 of US$ 7,600 placed China below Angola and Albania. China's GDP per capita, adjusted by purchasing power parity, reached US$ 7,517 in 2010, according to the International Monetary Fund. That's up from US$ 250 in 1980. Urban capita incomes are nearly three times higher than incomes in the countryside, according to data released by China's National Bureau of Statistics. In large cities, the gap is even more extreme. In 2008, Beijing's per capita GDP was US$ 9,085 while Shanghai's was US$ 10,529 in 2009.

A Deliberate Attempt to Undervalue the Yuan

An analysis undertaken by Manoj Pandit (*Economic Times* – November 11, 2011) reveals that there is a deliberate attempt by the Chinese government to undervalue its currency, the Yuan. Indicating the trade patterns of different countries and trade transactions in the past, the study concludes that China has become the manufacturing hub of the world. It keeps its Yuan down to export to developed countries which benefits from low priced goods. This move has also benefitted other Asian countries such as South Korea and Taiwan. If the value of Yuan rises suddenly, it will hurt consumers in the developed world and suppliers in Asia.

Acknowledgements

I acknowledge the support and help of Dr. Rupesh Pande, Faculty NIIT Beijing China for providing the required data and information.

Contributors' Profile

Hitesh Arora

Is an Associate Professor in the area of Quantitative Techniques/ Operations Management at FORE School of Management, New Delhi. A graduate in Mathematics and a post graduate in Operational Research from University of Delhi. He has also earned his Doctorate in Mathematical Programming from Department of Operational Research, University of Delhi.

Prof. Arora has qualified National Eligibility Test (NET) conducted jointly by CSIR & UGC for Lectureship with Junior Research Fellowship (JRF) in Mathematical Sciences. He started his teaching career from University of Delhi and taught subjects like Optimization, Queuing Theory, Inventory Management and Statistics besides guiding students in their project work. He has also worked as an Actuarial Consultant with a UK-based MNC. As an actuarial consultant, his work involved Data Modeling and Reserving for Personal and Commercial Lines of different UK-based insurance companies. He has over fourteen years of experience in academics and industry.

Prof. Arora has worked immensely in the area of Mathematical Programming. His present areas of research interest are Measurement of Productivity, Service Quality and Information Technology in Indian banking sector. He has to his credit, a number of research papers in national and international journals of repute. He has also conducted Management Development Programmes (MDPs) in Decision Making Techniques for Managers.

Prachi Bhatt

Is Assistant Professor in Organisation Behavior and Human Resources Management at FORE School of Management. She has around six years of experience in research and teaching. Her research experience and corporate association cover projects with Zydus Cadila Healthcare Ltd., Ahmedabad, GCMMF Ltd., Anand, Gujarat and Indraprastha Apollo Hospitals, New Delhi. She is certified in Negotiation Research and Teaching from Kellogg School of Management, Evanston & Chicago Campuses, USA. She has conducted workshops and MDPs for corporates from public and private sector organizations like Idea Cellular Ltd., ONGC Videsh Ltd., Biltech Building Elements Ltd., De La Rue Cash Processing Solutions India Pvt. Ltd., Apollo Tyres Ltd., and Uttarakhand Power Corporation Ltd.

Prof. Prachi's primary research and consulting interests include: Effectiveness in Negotiation, Negotiation Skills, Competency Mapping, and Changing HRD Paradigm. International Context of Negotiation, Organisation Behaviour, Human Resource Management, Business Ethics and allied areas are her secondary interests. The above mentioned areas are also the subjects that she teaches.

Ambrish Gupta

M.Com., Ph.D., FCA, CIT (IBFD, The Netherlands) Chartered Accountant.

Prof. Ambrish Gupta is a 'Rashtriya Gaurav' awardee. He has been teaching at FORE since 1997. Prior to that, he worked for 14 years in industry, mainly investment banking, as Director & Senior Vice-President. His teaching and research areas include Investment banking, Project financing, Financial accounting, Financial reporting standards, IFRS convergence and Contemporary corporate reporting practices. He has published **2 Books**, namely, *Financial Accounting for Management: An Analytical Perspective* (Pearson) and *Inflation Accounting: The Indian Context*, **18** papers, **4** working papers, **2** papers in the proceedings of international conferences in Germany and Macau (China) and **1** paper in an edited book. He has provided research guidance to **1** Ph.D. scholar and **40** major student projects.

Prof. Gupta is Co-editor – 'GSTF Business Review', Singapore, Member- Editorial board, 'Public and Municipal Finance', Ukraine and Program Committee of annual Conferences on Accounting and Finance, Singapore. He has attended faculty development programmes in China and Malaysia. He is a Fellow of ICAI, Member-Doctoral committee, Department of Management, Jamia Hamdard University, Capital market committee, PHD Chamber of Commerce and Editorial board, Rai Management Journal. He is a resource person for ICAI in many areas. His Papers have been presented in international conferences in Germany and Macau. He has authored a report on restructuring of FORE's PGDM curriculum, delivered talks on topics of his interest areas in MDPs and seminars including for IAAS officers and attended numerous seminars. He has been Chairperson (Finance) for 6 years and Programme Director (WMG) for 2 years at FORE.

Neetu Jain

Is Assistant Professor (OB/HRM), is MSc (Chem), MBA (HR) and has a doctoral degree from University of Banasthali. She holds Diploma in Training & Development from ISTD and has qualified UGC-NET. Recipient of 'AIMS International Outstanding Young Management Researcher Award' and 'Rashtriya Gaurav Award' 2009, she has thirteen years of teaching experience in reputed management institutes. She has also been an invited speaker in several forums of social concerns and conducted several MDP's on Stress Management, Anger Management, Cognitive

Reorientation, Meditation Sessions, and Mind Stilling Exercises. She teaches courses in organizational behaviour and human resource management at FORE School of Management.

Having a consistently good academic record, she has presented several papers in national and international conferences and contributed research papers to well known journals and periodicals. Her research work published in the form of a book titled "New Spiritual Foundations of Management" was released by Dr. Bengt Gustavsson, Stockholm University, Sweden in an international conference organized by Indus Business Academy, Greater Noida, in 2008. Her academic areas of interest include: Training and Development, Organisation Behaviour, Stress Management, Self Management and Indian Management Systems and Practices.

Anita Tripathy Lal

Has expertise in the areas of Business Communication, Leadership and Entrepreneurship. A PhD from IIT (Kanpur), she has over 16 years of work experience in the areas of teaching, training and research. Her experience of teaching includes three years as a visiting faculty at IIT (Delhi) and IIT (Kanpur). She has been a part-time consultant for two years to NTPC's World Bank funded projects on Environmental Impact Assessment.

She has keen interest in personality development and research related activities. Her research papers within the areas of Business Communication and Entrepreneurship have been well received in national and international conferences.

A proud recipient of the prestigious 'Mentor Development Programme for Entrepreneurs' jointly conducted by London School of Business and National Entrepreneurship Network. She has been successfully mentoring entrepreneurs. Her passion though, remains for student start-ups.

She has conducted a number of management development programmes (MDPs) for both Indian corporate and international participants. Some of the major MDPs are in the areas of Business Communication; Leadership Competencies and Entrepreneurship Development. Dr. Lal has been able to create an ideal blend of Leadership, Entrepreneurship and Communication in her training programmes, few of the most potential skills critical to creating success stories for organizations in today's uncertain times.

Shalini Kalra Sahi

Is an Assistant Professor in the Department of Finance and Accounting at FORE School of Management, New Delhi. She is a FPM from MDI, Gurgaon and her doctoral work has been in the area of Behavioural Finance.

She has around five years of experience in teaching at post graduate levels in management education. She has taught at Department of Business Economics, University of Delhi, Delhi, ICFAI Business School, Gurgaon and has also been associated as a guest faculty with IIT, Mumbai. Her teaching interests lie in the areas of: behavioural finance and financial decision making, investment management, financial accounting and corporate finance. She has a number research papers in both national and international journals. Her research interest lies in behavioural finance and investor psychology, qualitative aspects of money and finance, personality and gender issues in financial planning and management.

Mohita Gangwar Sharma

Is an electrical engineer from IIT-BHU, Varanasi and Masters in International Business from IIFT-New Delhi. She is a recipient of the coveted N.T.S.E. Scholarship.

She obtained her doctorate from Indian Institute of Management (IIM) Lucknow, making seminal contribution in the area of Spare Parts Management. Her industry profile includes a stint of over 4 years at BHEL, Bhopal, where she was involved in Product Designing, Manufacturing and Testing and ISO-9000 Activities. She worked in Indian Airlines in Materials Management Department for 10 years where she was involved with Tendering, Contract Execution, and Inventory Management Aspects of Supply Chain.

She has participated in National and International Conferences and has published papers. She brings the rich experience of the industry and tough academic rigor to her research. Her current areas of research include Operations Strategy, Product Service Systems, Supply Chain Intelligence and Service Operations.

Sanghamitra Buddhapriya

Is Professor and Area Chairperson in the area of Organizational Behaviour and Human Resource Management at FORE School of Management. She received the University Gold Medal for securing first class and first position in MA in Personnel Management & Labour Welfare. She has qualified the UGC-NET. She is a PhD from Faculty of Management Studies, University of Delhi. In 2001 she received the prestigious Indo-Canadian Faculty Research Fellowship and did her post-doctoral research from Mc Master University, Hamilton, Canada. She has authored two books and many of her research papers are published in national and international journals.

Her research interests are: Workforce Diversity; Gender Issues in Management; Work-life Balance and Stress Management and other related areas. In addition to these areas she provides consulting in the areas of Competency Mapping and Strategic Human Resource Management. She conducts Management Development Programmes in different aspects of Human Resource Management and Organizational Behaviour. Some of her successful training programmes are: Work-Life Balance for Women Executives; Leadership and Team Building; Interpersonal Skills at Work; Mentoring and Coaching; and Emotional Intelligence. She has carried out management development programmes/consulting assignments for organizations such as HPCL, MUL, EIL, NHPC, NTPC, MMTC, Power Grid Corporation, New India Assurance Company Limited and Aga Khan Foundation.

Asif Zameer

Is Associate Professor of Marketing at FORE School of Management. He is Bachelor of Engineering (Delhi College of Engineering), MBA (Jamia Millia Islamia) and Ph.D. (Jamia Hamdard University).

He brings with him more than 16 years of rich industry exposure and over 7 years of teaching experience. He started his career as an Engineer at BHEL, and later on moved into responsible positions in Marketing and Business Development areas for diverse organizations like Gillette, BHEL, Heatly & Gresham, Geep Torches and Amkette Computer Peripherals. He has taught Sales and Distribution, Retailing, Marketing Management, B2B Marketing, Mall Management, Supply Chain & Logistics at leading Business Schools in NCR. His research interests include Retailing, Mall-management, Sales & Distribution and Supply Chain Management and he has published a number of articles in leading international and national journals. He has conducted several seminars, MDPs and FDPs in the areas of Sales & Distribution, Marketing Research, Retailing and Supply Chain/Logistics.

Anupam Narula

Is Associate Professor in Marketing in FORE School of Management since February 2011. He has over 14 years of experience in teaching, training and research. Silver Medallist in PGDBM, he has taught in various premier B-schools in NCR like

Apeejay, Army Institute, Jaipuria, BIMTECH etc and had undertaken various institutional building activities with premier and upcoming B-Schools in NCR as Director, Dean, Officiating HOD, Founder and Coordinator for many new management programmes. His current teaching, consulting and research areas of interest include: Consumer Buying Behaviour, Strategic Brand Management, Service Marketing, Textile Marketing and Educational Marketing.

Vinay Dutta

Is a banker turned academician and a full time professor in the area of finance at FORE School of Management, New Delhi since September 2000. He is the recipient of Dewang Mehta Business School Award for Best Teacher in Financial Management during 2011.

Prof. Dutta started his career with Bank of India and has worked with Corporation Bank and Indusind Bank. He has almost two decades of banking experience mostly in trade finance. Before moving to Indusind Bank he also spent a year teaching at National Institute of Banking and Corporate Studies, Noida.

He teaches courses on management of commercial banks, personal wealth management and risk management to postgraduate students. He also regularly offers training programmes to senior corporate executives. He has research and consulting interest in the areas of banking, financial services, wealth management and risk management.

Himanshu Joshi

Is associated with FORE School of Management as Assistant Professor in the area of Finance and Accounting from last 3 years. He has more than a decade of experience in research and teaching at post graduate levels in Management Education. He has published and presented number of research papers in national/international conferences and refereed journals. He has successfully developed and delivered various management development programmes such as: finance for non-finance executives, advanced corporate finance, strategic financial management, and spreadsheet modelling for business valuation for reputed Indian companies and multinationals.

His areas of specialization include fixed-income securities, investment management, foreign exchange risk management and advanced corporate finance. His research and consulting interests lie in the areas of: management of FX operating and equity exposures, application of foreign currency debt and financial instruments like futures, forwards and currency swaps for FX risk management, valuation of fixed income and equity securities, performance evaluation of mutual funds, and financial engineering.

Neeraj Kumar

Has a total of 31 years, experience, 27 years in industry as a practicing HR Manager and an independent Consultant and 4 years in academia. He worked with SAIL for 24 years in different units in the HRM function. The major areas of his contribution were Performance Management, Organisation Development, Employee Relations Management, Training Solutions and internal consulting. He helped design and implement PMS and Strategic HRM interventions in large organizations in steel industry. As a part of an inter-disciplinary consulting team, he performed diagnostic studies in Egyptian Iron and Steel Company, Visweswaraiyya Iron and Steel Limited and recommended measures for management of change. He also designed and delivered customized training and management development programmes in organizations spread across public and private sectors on topics such as Strategic Management, Managerial Effectiveness, Soft Skills in Planning , Action-centered Leadership, Counselling and Coaching Skills, Domestic Enquiry and Discipline in Industry, Negotiations, Emotional Intelligence etc. He co-authored a text book entitled 'Employee Relations Management'.

Prof. Neeraj's areas of teaching interest include: Organisation Design and Change, Performance Management, Employee Relations (Industrial Relations) and Labour Legislations. His research interests are: Industrial Relations and Labour Legislation. And his consulting interests are: Performance Management and Management of Change.

Kanhaiya Singh

Has nearly three decades of experience in working with Canara Bank in various capacities including as Bank Economist. He took voluntary retirement from Canara Bank in March 2001 and joined academics.

Prior to joining FORE School of Management in January 2009, he was Associate Professor with Birla Institute of Technology (BIT), MESRA, Ranchi at its Noida Centre. He has more than 85 papers (including 12 research papers) published in the areas of banking, finance and economics in reputed national/international journals, books and leading financial papers. He also participated in various national/International conferences and presented research papers.

He has authored 7 books on various banking topics. A text book on "Commercial Bank Management" was jointly authored. One book on "Credit Policy" was written under the scheme of RBI. Four research scholars submitted Ph. D thesis at Birla Institute of Technology, MESRA RANCHI and another 2 are pursuing Ph. D under his supervision. He has conducted management development programme (MDP) on project finance, strategic cost management and financial derivatives.

Prof. Kanhaiya's areas of teaching include: management accounting, financial derivatives and financial services. He is a life member of Indian Economic Association and Indian Institute of Banking and Finance. His areas of research include: macroeconomic policy issues, impact and monitoring evaluation studies of social credit programmes, cost-benefit analysis, equity research, etc. The consultancy assignments involve: project evaluation and financial planning, capital structure and cost management and industry rehabilitation strategies.